SALVATION
YOUR PASSPORT TO HEAVEN

SALVATION
YOUR PASSPORT TO HEAVEN

DR. OLUSOLA ISRAEL FADARE

ReadersMagnet, LLC

Salvation: Your Passport To Heaven
Copyright © 2023 by Dr. Olusola Israel Fadare

Published in the United States of America
ISBN   Paperback: 979-8-89091-188-9
ISBN   eBook: 979-8-89091-189-6

All rights reserved. No part of this publication may be reproduced, stored in a retrieval system or transmitted in any way by any means, electronic, mechanical, photocopy, recording or otherwise without the prior permission of the author except as provided by USA copyright law.

The opinions expressed by the author are not necessarily those of ReadersMagnet, LLC.

ReadersMagnet, LLC
10620 Treena Street, Suite 230 | San Diego, California, 92131 USA
1.619. 354. 2643 | www.readersmagnet.com

Book design copyright © 2023 by ReadersMagnet, LLC. All rights reserved.

Cover design by Tifanny Curaza
Interior design by Dorothy Lee

TABLE OF CONTENTS

Dedication 7
Acknowledgements 9
The Original Sin 11
Preface 13
Introduction 17

CHAPTER ONE
What Does It Mean To Be Born Again? 19
CHAPTER TWO
The Greatest Question Ever Asked 24
CHAPTER THREE
Wrong Doctrine 30
CHAPTER FOUR
False Doctrine 31
CHAPTER FIVE
My 1st Heavenly Trip 33
CHAPTER SIX
What Is Salvation? 36
CHAPTER SEVEN
How I Got Born Again 41
CHAPTER EIGHT
Natural Birth And Spiritual Birth Compared 44
CHAPTER NINE
Know The Truth 50

CHAPTER TEN
The Cross Revisited 56

CHAPTER ELEVEN
Reasons Why People Get Saved 60

CHAPTER TWELVE
Sin, Sinners, And Divinity.. 65

CHAPTER THIRTEEN
The Almighty Jehovah God.. 71

CHAPTER FOURTEEN
What Jesus Did For The World 77

CHAPTER FIFTEEN
What To Do After Salvation 80

CHAPTER SIXTEEN
Forgiveness Is Not What You Think It Is 87

Book Summary 97
About The Author 99

DEDICATION

I humbly dedicate this book to the one and only Living God, the eternal Godhead who manifests Himself in three spiritual personalities. God the Father, the Son, and the Holy Ghost, and to one of the billions of souls saved by Jesus; my mother, Florence Adepeju, who went to be with the Lord in 1986.

ACKNOWLEDGEMENTS

I would like to wholeheartedly acknowledge the encouragement given by my wife and co-laborer in the ministry, Mercy Bukola, who kept reminding me to complete my writing projects – Ministerial and literary. Also, as the First Lady of The Living God Ministry in USA, for her leadership role and endurance. To our church Secretary an author herself who has been there from the beginning, Chinyere O. Onuwochuwkwa.

I am most grateful to the young Dr. Chiamaka E. Ahunna for her efforts and the arduous task of typing the manuscript.

Thanks to Stacey Gregory for initially bringing the manuscript into this amazing formation.

THE ORIGINAL SIN

Man was created and had all
Man sinned and lost all
by the original sin.
Glad, one died for all,
that all may be purged of sin.
You must be born again
You might not be born again in the USA
you can be born again anywhere
to possess a heavenly citizenship
To be born is secular
to be born again is spiritual
the natural birth is a miracle
the spiritual birth is a marvel.

Dr. OLU FADARE

PREFACE

I was born in Nigeria by divine providence, and by God's amazing grace, I was born again in the United States of America.

It sounds ironic that I was not saved in Nigeria but in the USA. The strong irony is that I escaped the new birth in southern Nigeria despite its huge concentration of fervent Christians, one of the largest in the world, to come to give my life to Jesus in America. This is America where there seems to be a solution to every problem, where there is the so-called almighty dollar for every need, a nearby doctor for every ailment, and your American dream on the horizon. Who will then wake up in the morning looking for how to get saved?

Conversely, an ordinary man in a developing country like Nigeria or elsewhere does not have the luxury of these things. For him, the common parlance is: **THE STRUGGLE CONTINUES**.

To some, half a century has passed, and it is still "**THE STRUGGLE CONTINUES.**"

A person in a developing or underdeveloped country has a much higher propensity to be born again than his counterpart in a developed country. He tends to have time for religious things and tends to listen when spoken to about God.

The aforementioned scenario is by no means a general rule of thumb. God can save anyone anywhere. Some, if not many, in griding poverty have been known to reject the saving grace of Christ, while many that live in affluence can be saved. That might be the reason I got saved by God's matchless grace in America. To be candid though, I was living pretty comfortably as a young budding banker in Nigeria.

I believe one should never forget the country of his birth and the country of his new birth. That is the country where he was born and the country where he was born again. For me, the first happened to be in Nigeria, a nation and people of great resilience and notable genetic smartness. The second happens to be in America, the land of the free, the home of the brave, the epitome of democracy, the bastion of capitalism, freedom, and liberty, the richest nation on earth, the land of inexhaustible dreams. Conversely, speaking, it is also the land that spiritually swallows up its inhabitants.

To be born again should have nothing to do with the wealth of a nation or an individual, but realistically it does. Again, generally speaking, an affluent person living in a wealthy country will be more inclined to trust in the vast resources around him than trust in God by faith.

Just what does it mean to be born again? How do you know you are born again, or someone close to you is born again? What are the misconceptions about salvation? Why must a person be born again before he/she dies, and is there hope for you or anyone that is not born again? A slow, reflective reading through this book will not only provide the answers to these and other questions but will impact your life and destiny here on earth and in heaven. Simply put, you will never be the same, whoever you are reading this book. Even if you are genuinely born again, sanctified and baptized by the Holy Spirit, this book will open up a new vista in your perception of the common salvation.

Ministers, pastors, evangelists, and those who love evangelism will find this book a ready resource in leading the unregenerated to Christ. I know for sure because the Lord has a purpose for strongly prompting me to write this book. He has given me inspirations and ideas and even scripture references. To Him, be glory incorruptible forever and ever.

I am not writing this because of my theological credential or my ministerial experience. Surely not because of my over 17 years of pastoral experience. My motive is not to make money either. In fact, I have vowed to God not to have a dime as gain or recover whatever money I might have spent writing and publishing this. It is all about simply obeying the Holy Spirit and a prophetic voice from a precious woman of God who lives 1,650 miles away from New York, my home State. She is not a prophetess, but she hears from God, "You will write a book. It will be on Salvation. Any unbeliever who reads this book will be saved." she had said. I was halfway into the manuscript when the quiet prophecy came over the phone. The amazing thing is that she did not say the book will be on deliverance or healing, knowing that God had called me into healing and deliverance ministry. Also, the fact that anyone who reads it will be saved. That exactly had been my most passionate prayer in the book. Wow! This was just the second time, at least, that she had come right down prophetic on my ministry, confirming about 8 years ago exactly what the Lord had told me on the future headquarters location of our church.

INTRODUCTION

Finding, owning, and reading this book is by no means an accident or mere chance. The best way to approach it and the best attitude to adopt is not to see or read it as a secular or fictional book. It is a serious, truthful and inspired book. It should also be read with a purpose. The purpose is, among many, to lead the reader to Christ through genuine salvation, to know that salvation is required to go to heaven after death, irrespective of a person's status or non-status in the society. These requirements are for kings, queens, presidents, billionaires, movie stars, music artists, celebrities, scientists, medical doctors, lawyers, teachers, students, plumbers, taxi drivers, street vendors, gays, and lesbians, male, female, transgender - you name it. All must be saved to make it to heaven.

A positive attitude of humility is essential when reading a book like this, especially those who are already saved. Without humility, one will display false pride and the inherent natural propensity to criticize the content of this book or downplay its benefits, thereby seeing it as good only for the unsaved or babies in the faith.

Allow me to say that I guarantee by the special grace of God that anyone who diligently reads this book as an unbeliever will be convinced that there is no other option but to repent and invite Jesus into their lives.

CHAPTER ONE
WHAT DOES IT MEAN TO BE BORN AGAIN?

To be born again, just what does it mean? Pardon me, I will start with what it means **NOT** to be born again, and then what being born again **DOES NOT** mean. They are two different things. I will explain momentarily. Read the poem below slowly and understandably.

> *"My life is in the yellow leaf*
> *All the flowers and youth of life are gone*
> *The worm, the canker, and the grief*
> *Are mine alone."*
> **Lord Gordon Byron.**

I call this the perfect POEM. One of the great, most powerful, and intriguing lines in the genre of poetry is the poem you have just read. Paradoxically, it is also one of the most pathetic and prophetic in all literary genres. It perfectly captured the agony of one of Britain's greatest poet's last hours on earth, written on his death bed.

This is what it means not to be born again. I happened to study Lord Byron and countless other great poets years ago as a university student of English and World literature. It has been some 34 years since I studied it in the university, and it has stuck to me since, rivaling some of the great works of William Shakespeare's plays that stuck with me. Can you envision a man in agony of pain and imminent death still able to pinpointedly, poetically, and powerfully captured the last vestiges of utter darkness and the agonizing prospect of the reality of the shadow of death in such incredible moving imagery.

This is what it means not to be born again.

It means hopelessness. It means what the metaphor of the yellow leaf means. In the fall season (autumn), the yellow leaf has lost its lush greenery, vigor and lusciousness, and is now losing its life. All the radiance is gone. It is in the last stage of witheredness as a lone, dry primrose in the wilderness and about to drop upon the lightest move of early morning breezes.

Lord Byron saw his diminishing life advancing into the shadow of death. He saw that shadow of death in that yellow leaf. The next stage would be death itself. He saw beyond death. He saw the pangs of death, the deserved punishment, or what I call the gates of hell. It is certain that at that point, the dying person sees beyond our realm; some see Angels waiting to take them up. Some see Jesus standing by, while some, like Lord Byron, saw the worm, the cankerworm, the grief, all depicting that terrifying place called hell.

Lord Gordon Byron (1788 - 1824) was the brilliant playboy poet of Britain. He enjoyed high life and women to the end. There was no thought of the need to be BORN AGAIN, but one day is appointed to meet his maker. Winston Churchill, prime minister of England during the 2nd world war, wrote:

"I am prepared to meet my maker; whether he is prepared for the ordeal of meeting me is what I don't know."

Was Churchill really prepared to meet God? Well, at least we know he knew there is a God, his creator. What we don't know is if he really prepared to meet him.

The only way to prepare to meet that God is by salvation. Speaking about Jesus, John in the New Testament wrote:

*"He was in the world,
and the world was made by Him,
and the world knew Him not.*

He came unto His own, and His own received Him not. But as many as received Him, to them He gave the power to become the sons of God, even to them that believe on His name which was born, not of blood, nor of the will of man, but of God."
(John 1:10 – 13)

Like Lord Byron, many today are not thinking about the salvation of their souls. Many have rejected Jesus and salvation, many are living and enjoying 'high life' with much money, women, ceaseless partying, booze, and all forms of reveling at the expense of their souls. The Bible is clear.

"For what shall it profit a man if he shall gain the whole world and loses his own soul? Or what shall a man give in exchange for his soul?"
(Mark 8:36 – 37)

If you really want to live or enjoy "high life," come to Jesus. The real "high life" is in Christ Jesus; without Jesus, what you are living is actually a low life – depriving yourself of the great peace in Jesus, the relationship, His love, the hope, the joy and happiness, the great knowledge and understanding of the world, the worldly system, the spiritual realm, the wonderful love of God, the plan of salvation, the precious word of God called the Holy Bible (the scriptures), the judgment that is hanging like the sword of Damocles over the head of Satan, and all who hate and reject Jesus and so on. These are some of the things you have deprived yourself of. Having known what it means NOT to be born again, let us briefly examine what being born again DOES NOT mean. This is where many, countless many folks have missed it. To be sure we are on the same page, Salvation. Born again. Saved. – these are the finished work of Christ on the cross for the redemption, of mankind from Satan's slavery, and from the inherited Adamic (from Adam) sin and its consequent death. There is physical death (separation of the spirit and soul from the body). The consequence of sin is not the physical death for sinners and saints who will all die one day. The presence and works of sin in a person without salvation will result in eternal death (separation of a person's soul and spirit from God forever and ever right after the physical death). That unrepented soul or unsaved soul is already spiritually dead by not knowing God.

> *"For the wages of sin is death but the gift of God is eternal life through Jesus Christ our Lord" (Romans 6:23)*

- Being born again or saved does **NOT** mean:
- Baptism in water only.
- Confession of sin without believing and inviting Jesus to your heart.
- Being religious.
- Going to church or any religious gathering regularly or being a member of a religious group since birth.
- Working in church or any religious organization during Saturday or Sunday services.
- Having Christian or biblical names.
- Saying the Lord's prayer, praying every day and reading the psalms.
- Praying daily and praying for your family and friends. Giving to charities and engaging in voluntary work.
- Being a nice person who bothers no one.
- Being honest and living a moral life.
- Staying away from crimes and trouble.
- Not having any vice-like drug or drinking habit.
- Fasting.

All of the aforementioned actions or activities do not make a person born again. Being born again or having salvation is not about doing this or not doing that. In other words, it is not by works. You cannot earn salvation. *(Titus 3:5)* says: *"Not by works of righteous which we have done, but according to His mercy He saved us, by the washing of regeneration, and renewing of the Holy Ghost."*

So then, what is it to be born again? I would say it is to be saved. And what is it to be saved? Well, let us consider some questions as we answer some of the questions I just posed.

CHAPTER TWO
THE GREATEST QUESTION EVER ASKED

In my estimation, the hardest, greatest though most relevant, and most fundamental question in all of life and eternity is one in the Bible.

> *"How shall we escape if we neglect so great a salvation? (Hebrew 2:3).*

Admittedly there are hard questions that mankind finds challenging. There are crises that elude resolutions and may never be resolved. For instance, whether there ever with be peace in the Middle East. Prime Minister Benjamin Netanyahu once made this immortal and factual statement:

"If the Arabs put down their weapons today, there would be no more violence, and if the Jews put down their weapons today, there would be no more Israel."

MORE QUESTIONS:

How can wars be eradicated in the world?

Is climate change real, and if so, what can be effectively done to combat it?

These are questions that concern nations, of the United Nations Organization, governments, and religious organizations because every nation will directly or indirectly be adversely impacted by the recurrence of war in the Middle East or the perpetuation of tensions and wars around the world. Yet one question, yes, one question that is more personal, more challenging, more relevant, and even more realistic is the question the Bible rhetorically asked:

HOW SHALL WE ESCAPE IF WE NEGLECT SO GREAT A SALVATION?

This question could be viewed as the greatest and, again, relatively most relevant question every adult person on earth should be asking or be asked. It is not an accidental or incidental question. It is a fundamental one. It is related to your life now and eternal FUTURE. In other words, not neglecting or dismissing the question now could enhance your chances of not neglecting the great salvation, and thereby your escape from the great white throne judgment sequel to eternity in the lake of fire.

HOW SHALL WE ESCAPE IF WE NEGLECT SO GREAT A SALVATION?

Escape what? You might ask. And what is that "great salvation?" Glad you asked because your life is about to be transformed. And if already, you are about to start changing other peoples' lives through the name of the Living God, the God of Abraham, Isaac, and Jacob, by the working of the Holy Ghost as you will be imparted with divine inspiration and deep revelation about the "great salvation" executed by the only potentate king of kings and Lord of lords – JESUS CHRIST our Lord.

NO ESCAPE

Allow me to state at this point that God Almighty did not prompt me to write this book so I can attempt to answer how to escape if we neglect or reject the great salvation. There is simply no way of escape. The answer to the seemingly rhetorical question is emphatically: No way of escape from judgement and hell if we neglect or ignore the great salvation. To be precise, there will be no escape from;

The coming wrath.

Let us go to the scriptures.

> *"But when he saw many of the Pharisees and Sadducees come to his baptism, he said unto them, O generation of vipers, who has warned you to flee*

> *from the wrath to come? Bring forth; therefore, fruits meet for repentance".*
> *"And think not to say within yourselves, we have Abraham to our father, for I say unto you that God is able of these stones to raise up children unto Abraham."*
> *Matthew 3:7-9 (King James Version). John 3:36 echoes the same theme.*
> *"He who believes on the Son has everlasting life, and he who believes not the Son shall not see life, but the wrath of God abides on him."*

And the apocalyptic book of Revelation 19:15 states:

> *"And out of His mouth goes a sharp sword, that with it He should smite the nations and He shall rule with a rod of iron, and He himself treads the winepress of the fierceness and wrath of Almighty God."*
> *Revelation 19:15.*

There will be no escape from: **Hell and The Lake of Fire.**

> *"And if your right eye offends you, pluck it out, and cast it from you, for it is profitable for you that one of your members should perish and not that your whole body should be cast into hell. And if your right hand offends you, cut it off and cast it from you, for it is profitable for you that one of your members should perish and not that your whole body should be cast into Hell".*
> *(Matthew 5:29-30)*

In the gospel of Mark, the same theme of hell is more expatiated and more graphic.

> *"And if your hand offend you, cut it off. It's better for you to enter into life maimed than having two*

> *hands to go into hell, into the fire that never shall be quenched, where their worm dies not, and the fire is not quenched".*
> *(Mark 9:43-44 KJV)*

Jesus Christ is speaking figuratively here. Your hand, your eyes could be anything so dear to you, just as the members of your body. For instance, if your profession or job makes you offend, it is better to quit it if quitting is the only way to avoid sin. If your hand literally makes you sin, and you decide to cut it off literally, you will lose your hand that could be used to do useful things. That is not a wise thing to do. Nonetheless, you will gain heaven. Jesus mentioned some people who became eunuchs, castrating themselves for the sake of the kingdom of God. *(Matthew 19:12).*

The kingdom of God allows violence (force, action). And the violent take it by force *(Matthew 11:12).* The metaphor of the eyes making one sin and having it plucked out is ironically an eye-opener. If you pluck them out, you have plunged yourself into utter darkness. Let us say you have in your possession a book, or books on Buddhism or Hinduism or witchcraft practice before you got born again. If you still read any of those books, and you want to heed Jesus' admonishment, and you literally pluck out your eyes, you will not only be able to read books of darkness that you still have but will have denied yourself the eyes to read the Holy Bible as well. Therefore, the wise thing to do will be to throw away those books and not your eyes.

When I got born again, I still had a stack of secular music C.D.s - sexually explicit songs, godless themed songs, marijuana-promoting songs, and others. I stopped listening to them without anyone telling me. My spirit, I would say the Holy Spirit in me, would not make me comfortable listening to them or desiring them any longer. Yet, I did not throw them away. When my wife wondered what they were there for without anyone playing them for months, my response was that I bought them with money, and it was hard for me to thrash them all. A couple of weeks or so went by, and it dawned on me that they would be there for the next ten years if I did not do something. The bible and gospel songs have replaced my collection and displaced my soul ties with them in my heart. If still stacked up, they could be useless for a while, but I could be tempted, or a visiting friend could one day play them. That might be a temptation to fall back into. I packed, bagged, and went straight to threw them all. I never looked back.

In our text in Mark 9 above, Jesus Himself described hell as a place where there is not only burning fire but where the fire is unquenchable. Why then there are some sects postulating some doctrines of their own philosophy that there is no burning hell but Gehenna. Gehenna is not hell. It is originally a grave. Hell is hell. Not only is the reality of hell proved for unrepentant sinners, but the wrath of God is also accentuated by something worse than hell: The Lake of Fire.

> *"And the sea gave up the dead which was in it, and death and hell delivered up the dead which was in them, and they were judged every man according to their works.*
> *And death and hell were cast into the Lake of Fire.*
> *This is the second death".*
> *(Revelation 20:13-14 KJV).*

When many people, including some sects, do not believe in hell, which is mentioned over 50 times in the entire Bible, how will they believe in the lake of fire? In the final judgment, as pointed out in the book of Revelation, death and hell including everything in hell – people who were once born again but died in a state of unrepented sin, people who rejected the gospel, people who rejected Jesus, wicked souls like Hitler and anyone who do not fear God, regardless of whether their crime is genocide, mass murder, serial killing, rape, habitual lying, hatred of other people and so on, shall be cast from hell into something worse - endless torment in the lake of fire.

Know also that demons and their master Satan who would already be in hell at that time would also be cast into the lake of fire. At this point, I would like to plead with readers not to dismiss any of these scriptural truths. Anyone writing a scriptural book like this must be careful not to misrepresent God's truth. It will be tantamount to misleading innocent souls. One cannot and should not cover up the truth and expound lies or misinterpretations either.

Well, what about a writer (author) who sincerely misrepresent the truth due to their shallow spiritual understanding of the word of God? No doubt, there are hundreds of preachers who fall into that category. Unfortunately, such might have been infected by their denominational background – by the doctrine, they were born into and raised by. So, is it their fault?

The Lord will have mercy if their doctrine does not mislead as to cause people to stumble or forsake the faith. The Bible is clear:

> *"Whosoever, therefore, shall break one of these commandments and shall teach men so, he shall be called the least in the kingdom of heaven, but whosoever shall do and teach them, the same shall be called great in the kingdom of heaven."*
> *(Matthew 5:9).*

A person can sincerely teach or write what they believe is the truth of the scripture, but he or she can also be sincerely wrong.

CHAPTER THREE
WRONG DOCTRINE

There are those who teach wrong doctrines. There are those who teach false doctrines.

There are those who teach heresy. For the purpose of explanations, let us use the scripture in **Luke 14:27** as example.

"And whosoever doth not bear his cross and come after me cannot be my disciple."

If a teacher or a pastor teaches his church members to each have a physical wooden cross and carry it literally on their shoulders wherever they go, making it clear that the cross should be at least the same height as the carrier of it and must not be less than 15 pounds by weight, that will be pretty uncomfortable for anyone to be carrying about. Suppose his congregation follows the pastor's interpretation of this scripture, each bringing his/her own cross to church. Do you know that the congregation will likely obey him, thinking they are obeying Jesus? Before you know it, they will be defending their actions. They will make people realize that Jesus literally carried his cross, an emblem of suffering and death. Before long, the church in question would have made a doctrine of it. Friend, that is an example of the wrong doctrine. I believe no one would go to hell because of that so long as they were genuinely born again and walk the Christ-like walk of faith. But then all that is much ado about nothing. It is unnecessary.

CHAPTER FOUR
FALSE DOCTRINE

For those who teach false doctrine, it is a little weirder and more serious. Let us use this scripture for our example.

> *"If any man come to me and hate not his father and mother, and wife and children and brethren and sisters, yea, and his own life also, he cannot be my disciple.*
> *Luke 14:26 KJV.*

Imagine an evangelist, teacher, or pastor teaching that you or anyone who is a disciple of Christ (simply means Christians) or wants to be born again and be a Christian must hate their Father, siblings, mother, have nothing to do with them but just come to Jesus and focus on Jesus only. And that the disciple must also hate himself/herself. If he is sick, he should not bother to go to the doctor or pray for healing. He should hate himself to the extent of not minding what he eats, whether a healthy diet or not. He is just lost in Jesus.

Do you know there are sects that teach this false doctrine with variations depending on their leader? Surely, when you are in such a congregation or group, they will convince you by rightly elevating Jesus as the only object of your love and affection. They will preach other things about Jesus right: that He is your Savior, He died in your place, He suffered and shed His precious blood for you, He loves you to death. Before you know it, you will be literally hating the people Jesus wants us to love, whereas that scripture has just been misinterpreted. It cannot mean hate as in the feeling of intense personal dislike for. Jesus would not contradict Himself or His Word, the Bible.

The Scripture in Luke 14:26 means that you will have to "love less" your parents, your siblings, etc. if you want to love Jesus much. Otherwise, there would be divided loyalty. Jesus will not have anyone compete for our first love, which is God.

False doctrine could also be seen in the teaching of some denominations that the Holy Spirit came in the first century in the Book of Acts and left in the first century in the book of Acts. So if you see people in church speaking in tongues and working miracles, they surmise it is not the Holy Spirit. They even go to the extent of asking their audience to run away from such, that it is not the spirit of God they are using. They perfectly misinterprete what Apostle Paul wrote in 1 Corinthians 13:8-10

"Charity never faileth: but whether there be prophecies they shall fail; whether there be tongues, they shall cease; whether there be knowledge, it shall vanish away. For we know in part, and we prophesy in part. But when that which is perfect is come then that which is in part shall be done away".

The false doctrine preachers or teachers teach that tongues have ceased. Meaning, speaking in tongues (unlearned and unknown language) has ceased in the church. Prophecy, and miracles, according to them, have vanished away.

I will not mention the church denominations that teach this false doctrine. Paul warned the church in **_Galatians 1:6-9_** and **_2 Corinthians 11:3-4_** *of false perverts.*

Going back to our scriptures of 1 Corinthians 13:8-10, it simply means that love (charity) will continue in heaven while prophecy will not be needed in heaven. Same with speaking in tongues and knowledge. In heaven, we will have just one universal language and will know much things without learning.

CHAPTER FIVE
MY 1ST HEAVENLY TRIP

On January 3rd, 2011, I had a dream that I was caught up in the third heaven. I found myself in a group of Saints and angels floating in the air from one point to another point. I deliberately used the word "floating" because we were not walking. Flying would have been another appropriate word to use, but we didn't have wings, and we were not flapping our arms either. My point is that prophet Samuel was in the group as all of us, about 50, floating in the air, moving as exactly as military jets fly during America's 4th of July Air show. That was how we were floating. No one surged even 6 inches ahead of any in the group. No one told me that prophet Samuel was there. I just knew. I did not even bother to look to my left where his position was. Every one of us was important as Samuel or any other Saint.

In heaven, we will have ready knowledge of most things. In this world, we will still need learning and knowledge, prophecy, and tongue-speaking.

HERESY

The third category of error is heresy. It is the worst of the other two, that is, wrong doctrine and false doctrine. Heresy is described as a belief or opinion contrary to orthodox Christian doctrine. In our example of wrong doctrine teachers earlier, we saw that a wrong doctrine teacher might interpret carrying your cross as physically carrying a wooden cross. So, he teaches his listeners or congregation to do so.

The wrong doctrine teacher misinterprets that scripture in Luke 14:27 and teaches people his wrong doctrine. We also discussed the example of false doctrine teachers that say there is no longer baptism of the Holy Spirit with its initial evidence of speaking in tongues. If they do not believe in post - New testament tongue-speaking, then they cannot believe in Holy Ghost baptism because that experience has always had the evidence of speaking in tongues. They go further (some of them) that anyone who spoke in tongue ceased in the New Testament. Again, this teaching is false teaching.

The wrong doctrine teacher may still be in the kingdom and in the faith, as a servant of God, but he is unnecessarily shortchanging himself by not denying himself and carrying his cross (spiritually speaking) as taught by Jesus. Jesus even said such cannot be His disciples unless they carry their cross and follow Him.

The false teacher is worse in that even though he is still in the kingdom (in the faith), he will never fulfill or get to his destiny in Christ. If he is to be used by God to work miracles, healings, and deliverance, he will never fulfill that calling because no one can do all those works without the Holy Spirit. If by faith he does some healings and deliverance, it will be a tiny fraction of what he would have done with the power of the Holy Spirit.

The one who teaches heresy is the worst of the three scenarios. Examples of heretic doctrines can be seen in religious sects or preacher:

- That believe not in the Trinity of God the Father, God the Son (Jesus), and God the Holy Spirit. God is one God with three distinct personalities but the same attributes - invisible spirits, omnipotent (can do all things), omniscient (knows all things), and omnipresent (present everywhere).
- That does not teach salvation of souls as in

> *" Except a man is born again,*
> *he cannot see the kingdom of God." John 3: 3b*

- That preach that there is nothing like Salvation, that everyone is saved already, or that you do not need Salvation.

- That Jesus cannot save anyone because he was just a prophet and everyone has to save himself/herself.
- That Jesus is not the only begotten son of God and that God has no Son.
- That Jesus is not coming back to take His saints in rapture, or that Jesus had come already.
- That Jesus did not die for anyone, or that He did not resurrect, or He is not alive.
- That there is no hell or Lake of fire.
- That you should not believe everything in the Bible because, they say, the Bible is not complete or written by men.

There are many more. A person that is born again (saved), genuinely born again, and reads, studies and hears the Bible truly taught will know right away if there is heresy in someone else's statement, belief, or teachings.

A heretic person is completely out of the Kingdom (not in the faith). If it is a church, sect, or religious group, you can rightly call them a cult. Salvation cannot be better described than what the Bible, the great word of God, has taught. There is nowhere in the Bible where we are taught an academic definition of Salvation. But we have several scriptures that tell us how to get saved and a perfect picture and scripture of what Salvation is.

CHAPTER SIX
WHAT IS SALVATION?

The perfect picture of Salvation or a Saved person is presented to the world in the 2nd book of Corinthians. **11 Corinthians 5:17** as follows:

Therefore, if any man be in Christ,
he is a new creature.
Old things are passed away;
behold all things are (have) become new.

Salvation is being in Christ. It does not say if any man is in Church or in the singing choir. As good and indispensable as the Church is, it is not the harbinger of Salvation. You may not get saved in Church, but you must be in Church to stay saved. I will expatiate further on the mandatory requirement of being a member of the body of Christ in the course of this book.

Let me break it down more. The passage of the verse quoted above further says that a person who is now in Christ "is a new creature." That is, the independent clause, he is a new creature, means simply what it says. It implies that the person used to have different character or characteristics from what he now has. These characteristics are so different and all-encompassing that one can categorically say "this person is a new creation" or "he or she is a totally different person." The person who uses the phrase "is a new creature" or the clause "he is a new creature" does no longer see any part of the old characters in the saved person. If he sees, he will have said, "he is partially a new creature or almost a new creature. In the same vein, the one who describes the saved person as a totally different person will not have so described him if he sees many new characteristics and only a few old ones. That is why he does not describe the saved person as a somehow different person or somewhat different character. He says he is a totally new person. These are actually how people describe their relatives, friends, or church members who just got born again. "Oh, she is now a new person," Let us examine the rest of the scripture we are dealing with.

Old things have passed away, behold all things have become new. The truth is that everyone who lives with, works with, or comes into contact with a saved person will know or notice that the old ways of life have passed away. They will also notice that all things have become new.

SCRIPTURAL BAROMETER.

You can call **2 Corinthians 5:17** the scriptural barometer or spiritual scale of Salvation.

Therefore, if any man is in Christ, he is a new creature: old things have passed away, behold all things have become new. This beloved scripture we have been dealing with is a **ONE WAY** Scripture in **APPLICATION**. I mean, it applies to someone who got born again who used to be "an unbeliever" or "in the world." The Bible calls him/her a sinner or the wicked, or the unregenerate or a fool, or the unrighteous. Those who are genuinely, truly born again are righteous, Saved, believers, regenerated, Saints.

The men and women of God in the entire Bible that are now in heaven are saints. The word saints is also used to refer to or describe the living Saints - those who are true children (men and women) of God that are in churches (Bible-preaching churches). They live a Christ-like life of consecration, holiness and love, believing and waiting for that blessed hope and the glorious appearing of our Lord and Savior, Jesus Christ. I am one of them by the Grace of God. You should be one of them if you are not. Right now. Friend, do not be deceived or self-deluded about Salvation. Perhaps you are not sure you are really saved. You might need to come anew to the cross again, that is, sincerely repent and confess all known sins. Ask for forgiveness and invite the Spirit of Jesus to come into you. There are a great number of people in the Church who are not truly born again. They are like those out in the world who are real people or famous celebrities who believe there is God, do go to church when it is convenient or they get too busy to go, but sing at events and funerals:

"Amazing Grace, how sweet the sound that saved a wretched like me. I was once lost, but now I see." Can you hear how sweet that truly sounds? Yet it is not a substitute for Salvation, and many sing it though they are still lost, still blind spiritually and still wretched.

Old things have passed away, behold all things have become new. If you or anyone still finds a trace of the old lifestyle in you, what do you do? Do you say, oh, I really have not been born again, or I do not think I can ever know how to be born again? Perhaps you might even give up altogether. It is very important that you note the difference between still having traces of the old life in you and committing sin after you have been saved. There are two different things.

COMMITTING A SIN

A saved person, if not careful to guide his salvation experience jealously, can transgress the commandment of God. In fact, sin is defined as the transgression of the law according to the scripture in 1st John. ***Whosoever committed sin transgresseth also the law: for sin is the transgression of the law (1 John 3:4 KJV).***

In modern English, committeth will be 'commits.' The scripture could be better put in this way: anyone who has committed sin has transgressed (broken) the law. "Whosoever" or anyone here is referring to a Christian. If a person has never been saved, he is not described as having committed a sin even if he just committed one. He is considered a sinner living in sin. He is living a life of sin, open or hidden sin. He needs to genuinely repent, confess his sinful life in remorse, acknowledge Jesus as the only one who can save him, invite Jesus to his life while forsaking his sinful life. He needs to make a total U-turn and start to live the Christian life that made the disciples (followers) of Jesus 'Christians" first in Antioch. **(Acts 11:26)**.

But a Christian who committed a sin only has to genuinely repent of that sin, forsake it and quickly go back to living the Christian life called the **CHRISTLIKE LIFE**.

HAVING TRACES OF OLD LIFE

Remember, we are trying to distinguish between a believer who committed a sin and the one whose behavior exhibits traces of the old canal life.

In this scenario, say, a believer (Christian) manifests visible anger as an emotional reaction to a situation. This does not mean he has sinned. He is just showing his old man. That does not mean everything is alright, and life should continue as usual when he recovers from his fit. No. He will need to deal with his anger; otherwise, he will sin with it by punching someone in the face or cursing out someone with profane, verbal expression.

He can deal with his anger by muttering self-control, remaining silent, or walking away from a tense situation. The best approach in dealing with his anger is to call upon God to take it away. He will have to do his own part by rejecting anger in his life, the more he reads and studies the Bible with consistency.

Salvation is not just baptism in water, contrary to what many who are really not born again think. I was taught in the late 1980s that Christians have to witness Jesus Christ so sinners can make decisions and be born again. When we teamed up or paired up to do just that, we called it evangelism.

From the first day that we practiced it in the community, I was fascinated with it so much that I started to do it on my own, in what is called personal evangelism. Some of us young people at that time were timid, too timid to talk. But they could hand out little tracts. There was no problem as long as the strangers accepted them. If refused, some brethren (brothers and sisters in the Lord) became ashamed and got timider. They never wanted to hand out tracts any longer, talk less of talking. For those who were bold enough to talk, all we had to do was to share our individual testimonies of Salvation. If you are truly saved, you must have a testimony of who you used to be and how you got transformed by the finished work of Jesus Christ on the cross a little over two thousand years ago.

Some of our testimonies were dramatic. I mean, how Jesus saved them from the hopeless, careless, sinful life they had lived, onto a new life of repentance and forsaking of sinful life and acceptance of new life of righteousness and Christ-likeness. Then baptism in the water comes after. It could be the same day or any day in the near future, depending on the circumstance of the place where Salvation took place - home, street, church, or at a Christian mass crusade.

When I say some testimonies of Salvation were dramatic, I mean someone hearing the message of Salvation, that is the preaching of the cross, which is the gospel, might be praying right there as he was sitting or standing in a very loud voice, confessing his or her sin and asking for the mercy of God to forgive and cleanse him. Another might be sobbing uncontrollably, unmindful of the crowd around him, asking for the Salvation of his soul.

CHAPTER SEVEN
HOW I GOT BORN AGAIN

I will always remember my own experience back in December of 1988. Before this time, I had been in a church for almost four years, but I was not actually born again. The reason is that the Church neither preached nor understood Salvation. As they say, you cannot grow above your Church. Nobody understood the concept of Salvation or ever talked about it. All we knew, including the leaders, was dance to the songs with the choir, sing along with the choir (and they were good praise songs to listen to), read of a bible passage, take offerings (another time of dancing), listen to the announcement, listen to the message from the pulpit by the leader in-charge of the Church or one of the leaders or prophets and then end the Sunday service by reciting the Grace in *2corinthians 13:14*

The Grace of our Lord Jesus Christ and the love of God, and the communion of The Holy Ghost be with you all. Amen.

During preaching time, the message was almost always filled with personal stories, accusations against another leader or leaders who had been overtly fraudulent outside of the Church, personal vendetta against another leader with whom the preacher, in adulterous relationship had clashed over a young lady. At best, the preaching would be more on mere morality than spirituality.

As you should guess, every Sunday in Church was partly used to resolve conflicts or mediate in some matters between foes. If there was no knowledge of Salvation, do not expect an altar call on any service day- Wednesday evenings, Friday evenings, and Sunday mornings. There was never one altar call. Never.

When I separated from that Church, I was invited to another one. By that time, I had just been married to a young lady who had been born again some six months earlier. In fact, this new Church happened to be a New York branch of the Church she had been born again. Both of us were invited. We honored the invitation. I had to because my wife had once reluctantly gone with me to my old Church. It was my turn now to try hers.

The message preached that Sunday afternoon was so different and Bible-based that I just could not return to my old church the following Sunday. I had been convicted in my Spirit in the new Church but not been actually saved. At least I had known the difference between light and darkness, between knowledge and ignorance. That was in the summer of 1988.

Then came December of 1988. A guest minister came to our new Church from another state. He was actually the national pastor of our new Church, residing and overseeing all the four or five churches, including ours, from his headquarters in Montgomery, Alabama.

We had a special, retreat-like program in Church in a long service with periodic break time. After a powerful message was preached, it was time to eat a free, prepared or catered variety of food and snacks. There was no one left in the sanctuary hall except me. The way the message got into me left me no consideration of venturing to get on the food line. I knew I did not eat before going to Church, but the message of the cross took away my appetite altogether. I was like someone who had been dealt a knockdown blow. Food was like nothing to me but punishment. So I did not even think of saving it till a later time.

I looked around. The other congregants were either online for food or outside of the premises. I would not know if there were some three or four people like me who would not eat. This is different from a person who had purposed to fast during the day's retreat. My own circumstance was a person who would have in all certainty eaten, but the word of life, the gospel message, had taken away my appetite. As I was trying to ponder on what had happened to me, perhaps trying to make sense of it and recover, I saw the preacher still on the podium, sitting behind the pulpit, perhaps waiting to counsel anyone who would request counseling. I got up, painstakingly took steps towards him as if it would be sinful or too careless of me walking otherwise. In fact, I did not even have the strength, or I thought I did not have the strength to walk less gingerly.

"Sir, I never met you before," I croaked out the words like a frog stranded on dry land, "but I have never heard anything like that in my life." He looked at me and said without any emotion, "Is that so?"

SAME SALVATION, DIFFERENT PERCEPTION.

If you are born again, your own experience of Salvation may not have been eventful or dramatic as described above; nonetheless, it should still be an unforgettable one.

CHAPTER EIGHT
NATURAL BIRTH AND SPIRITUAL BIRTH COMPARED

Allow me to use the analogy of natural birth to explain a point about the new birth. The birth of a baby anywhere in the world is always not a quiet occurrence.

- It is marked with great joy.
- It is new. The same single incident never happened before.
- It is shrouded in mystery. How the baby starts eating, fed with milk to survive and to live.

Some things must have taken place in the mother's womb before the birth; if those things, including the biological process, did not take place or not completed, a stillborn may ensue.

The baby does not keep quiet after birth but cries and cries.

In Nigerian culture, especially in southern Nigeria, it is regarded as strange if a new born baby is not crying. So the midwife or a family member of the mother will slap the baby gently on the thigh or throw her up to catch her. Then the baby cries, and the family members get no little pleasure.

From the time of delivery, the relationship between the mother and the baby actually starts. She now talks to the baby, kisses her or him apart from caring for all the baby's needs. The baby is totally dependent.

In the new birth Christian experience, there are similarities and contrasts.

It is also marked with joy. The folks around the person who has just had a change of heart (repented) and has received Jesus Christ into his heart (born again) rejoice. The peace and joy in his heart are from the inside out. He feels so relieved as if a heavy burden has been lifted off him, and the joy is unspeakable. He cannot express it with laughter, dance, or any outward manifestation. He feels like a billionaire though he may be as poor as a compulsive gambler who just lost it all.

It is a new experience. The same experience never happened before.

It is a mystery, having nothing changed in his body, yet everything inside of him has changed.

Something must have taken place inside of him, in his heart, soul, and Spirit. As the natural birth, if those things inside of him (heart, soul, Spirit) did not take place, or just partially took place, a spiritual stillbirth would ensue. The person is dead on arrival, though physically, he is alive. It would appear he never was born again because the only thing he probably did was to say the sinner's prayer after a minister.

The new man does not keep quiet following his spiritual new birth but begins to pray and pray without being pushed. Just like the real-life baby (newly born) cries to communicate his feelings and needs, the born-again man communicates his needs through prayer.

From the time of Salvation of his soul, the relationship between him and God actually starts. It does not matter how old he is or how long he has been going to Church, he just starts a relationship with God.

The Lord now talks to him in dreams, visions, from reading and studying the word of God (The Holy Bible) and other means of communication God uses. The new man in Christ starts to trust God and depends on God. That is what God wants, for His children to trust him and depend on his provisions.

Trust in the Lord with all
Thine (your) heart; and lean not
Unto thine own understanding.
In all thy (your) ways acknowledge
Him and he shall direct thy path (Proverbs 3:5 &6)

CONTRAST

Interestingly there are contrasts between natural birth and spiritual births.

Natural birth takes place as a result of conjugation between a man and a woman. They both reproduce a baby between them. Babies can be born out of wedlock, but biblically speaking, it has to be in wedlock.

Spiritual birth is not by conjugation. It is not reproduced but produced by faith in Jesus Christ. Jesus Christ, the son of the Living God (Matthew 16:16), left His heavenly glory, took the form of a man so He could redeem mankind from his sin and the recompense (reward) of sin, which is death. Except you are a Christian, truly born again, you might ask questions like why man has to be redeemed from the slavery and captivity of sin? If so necessary, that man must be redeemed; why couldn't Jesus or God just come or say something and get us redeemed? After all, He can do all things as Christians claim?

In the course of this book, there will be common questions and answers so the person who is contemplating coming to the saving Grace of God through Salvation of his or her soul may know that to be born again makes sense, and there is nothing in the Bible and in the Christian faith that is vague or lies, or dark or opaque. Every truth and doctrinal truth is transparent.

To answer the likely questions posed above, man (generically referring to mankind) had to be redeemed from the captivity of sin. The captor is Satan. Man had become slaves to Satan. As slaves and captives, man cannot free himself. He is bound to do the will of his captor. In that state of man, he wallows in the deep water of sin.

In the end, he is drowned. Death ensues. Spiritual death ensues, as the Bible says in

(Romans 6:23)
For the wages of sin is death
But the gift of God is eternal life
Through Jesus Christ our Lord.

God cannot just say something or Jesus come down to earth, do something to redeem us from the evil hands of Satan and the clutch of death, and then fly back to heaven. Does a person live to be 2000 years before dying? By choice or design, no one lives up to that. Does a soldier jump down from a jet plane at 32,000 feet altitude without a parachute? The answer to this is also no. The jumper must have studied something about the force of gravity. He must have known there are principles he has to follow to be able to jump down safely. In the same vein, there are spiritual laws and principles. One of them is in Hebrews 9:22.

And almost all things are by the law purged with blood. And without the shedding of blood is no remission (forgiveness) of sin.

In all of the old Testament books from Genesis to Malachi, it had been ordained that the blood of animals, through sacrifices, had to be offered for the sin of individuals. The life of the flesh is in the blood.

"For the life of the flesh is in the blood:
and I have given it to you upon the altar
to make atonement for your souls:
for it is the blood that maketh an atonement
for the soul." (Leviticus 17:11)

Atonement is reparation for a wrong or injury. It is part of making amends. If we know anything about the Israelites, they offered sacrifices upon sacrifices through priests and chief priests. Do not confuse Israelites with Israelis. The Jews of modern-day Israel are Israeli. The animals for sacrifice must be perfect in appearance, with no blemish or spots. There was also a paradigm of national atonement whereby a goat would be presented, called the SCAPEGOAT. The scapegoat would not be killed like other goats and animals. It would be loosed to escape into the woods. God, Jesus, and the Holy Spirit in heaven accepted animal sacrifice in the old covenant. But then it pacified them, not really satisfying for the cleansing of sinners. It cleansed only the flesh.

Something better than the blood of animals, something more efficacious, something purer and more perfect, would be needed to satisfy. No man was worthy of satisfying the condition because of the inherently depraved nature of man incidental to his Adamic sin. Angels of God are sinless, but none would volunteer to come incarnate, that is, take the form of man and be ready to carry all the sin of the world. And the shame. What about the sufferings? But praise to our Lord, Jesus volunteered Himself. He gave Himself up.

As the only begotten son of the father, it was the toughest decision for God to give Jesus up and allow Him to come to the World as a propitiation for the sins of the World. God must have loved Jesus so much that He would have sent some other heavenly citizen if there was anyone perfectly clean and willing. God also loved the world so much that He sent His only son **(John 3:16)**. He would come, and He would die, shedding His blood. When the perfect (Jesus) came, the imperfect (animals sacrifice) was done with. He shed His blood. Remember, without the shedding of blood, there is no remission (forgiveness) of sin. If Jesus had been thrown into the sea to die, if He had been starved to death, if He had been choked, all or any of these would not have resulted in bloodshed, and He would not have been able to purge our sin.

> *"For if the blood of bulls and of goats, and the ashes of a heifer sprinkling the unclean, sanctifies to the purifying of the flesh:*
> *How much more shall the blood of Christ, who through the eternal Spirit offered Himself without spot to God, purge your conscience from dead works to serve the Living God?"* **(Hebrews 9: 13-14)**

The scripture quoted above in plain English expresses that if the mere sprinkling of unclean and defiled persons with the blood of sacrificed goats (and bulls) and with the ashes of a burnt heifer (a young female cow that has never given birth) was sufficient for the cleansing and purification of the body, the flesh, then how much more shall the blood of Jesus Christ, who through the eternal Spirit offered Himself without blemish to God, cleanse your conscience from dead works to serve the Living God?

CHAPTER NINE
KNOW THE TRUTH

Jesus left His glory above to come to the earth as a human to die for our sins. God cannot die. He had to take the form of a man because God cannot die. It is called incarnation. He never relinquished His divinity but became human, so human as if He was never divine and so divine as if He was never human. Without the former, He would not have been able to relate with mankind, mixing with people, meeting their needs, suffering for the sin and dying, and without the latter, He would not have been able to defeat the devil on all fronts. He would not have been able to destroy the work of the devil and be victorious.

THE JEWISH QUESTION

In the winter of 2004, the movie the PASSION OF CHRIST came out. Then the controversy about who killed Jesus became universal. Christian and secular magazines did the analysis, wrote comments and commentaries. The famous Christian magazine **CHARISMA** not only made the subject their lead Articles but also published readers' letters. Some of them accused the Jews of killing Jesus. Many, with the undertone of hate, handed down outright condemnation to the Jews. Of all the accusers, none to my recollection exonerated even the modern-day Jews. Now you wonder why so much spate of anti-Semitism in our society.

My own contribution, published by **CHARISMA**, endeavored to correct the notion that the Jews killed Jesus. By putting facts and history in their correct perspective, I wrote to the effect that Jesus had to come to the world to save mankind. To accomplish the great task, He must die. He is the sacrificial lamb that must die. This is embedded in the plan of Salvation. True, a number of Jewish leaders, the chief priests, and the scribes instigated a conspiracy against Jesus because they saw Him as a threat to their social standing in the society and everything they stood for in religion. They only had to stir up the common men. Before you know it, bang! The nails are on the cross, and Jesus is on it between the nails and the cross.

While many Jews were bent on having Jesus killed, some Jews believed in Him – during His Ministry, during His trial and crucifixion, and after His death, burial and resurrection. Remember Joseph of Arimathea, a wealthy Jewish man, asked for Jesus' body to bury Him. So, why hate the Jews? Do you know if Jesus did not die the vicarious death, you and I would not be saved? Never. We would have to die for our sins - physically, spiritually, and eternally. Then Jesus would not be called the **SAVIOR** of the world, and no human would have been able to save himself, talk less of saving the world.

There was no single sheep, goat, bull, or any animal for sacrifice that died by killing itself. For Jesus to die for the sin of the world, He would not have killed Himself. Like the animals sacrificed, He had to be killed. The great difference remains that every animal that was killed for sacrifice in Bible days did not want to die. Try it with any animal. Before you slaughter it for food, it will give you the fight of its life. It will struggle. It will let out the cry of its life. But Jesus submitted Himself. No vilification when He was vilified; they railed on Him, reviled Him, spat on Him. The Bible says He reviled not back. No struggle, no self-pity for His self-Sacrifice on the altar of Salvation.

YOUR NAME IS IN THE BIBLE

When I say your name is in the Bible, I do not mean because you are named Joshua, Michael, Rachel, or Joseph. Whatever your name is, even names like Frank, Henry, Smith, Darlene, April, Wood, Sade, Bisi, Hernandez, Kate, Spade, Doris, Allen, Ronald, Wright- whatever is your name, it is in the Bible. It may be an Italian name, Jewish, Arabic, Irish, African, Jamaican, French, and on and on; I will show it to you here in this passage:

> *He came unto His own, and His*
> *Own received Him not,*
> *But as many as received Him,*
> *To them gave He power to become*
> *The sons of God, even to them*
> *That believes in His name. (John 1:11-12)*

Your name is in line 3. Jesus was not generally accepted and received by the Jews. He was largely rejected.

"But as many as received Him."

That is, you if you have received Him or you are ready to receive Him. The Living God had you in mind whether you are a member of a church, mosque, synagogue, Hindu temple, Buddhist temple, or you do not belong to any of these. Suppose you can only receive the one that died for your sin so you can be saved from sin, death, and hellfire. As many as received Him, He, God, He, Jesus gave them the power (the right) to become sons and daughters of God.

Let us look at **verse 13,** the next verse of the scripture quoted above:

> *Which were born, not of blood,*
> *Nor of the will of the flesh,*
> *Nor of the will of man, but*
> *Of God. (John 1:13)*

Another contrast between natural birth and spiritual birth is expressed in the scripture quoted above. The person that is born again was not born again of flesh and blood (human) or by the working or action of man. It is the will and work of God.

NICODEMUS, THE IGNORAMUS

Nicodemus was a ruler of the Jews. He was probably a member of the trustee of a synagogue or perhaps a member of the political ruling council. He was a dignitary. He visited Jesus by night, secretly to ask questions about Salvation. Jesus, by the gift of prophecy or word of knowledge, discerned the thought of his mind. He was only acknowledging Jesus as Rabbi (teacher) sent by God, when Jesus right away gave him the answer to the question of his heart:

> *Verily, verily (truly) I say unto you,*
> *Except a man is born again,*
> *he Cannot see the kingdom of God. (John 3:3)*

Jesus was astounded that Nicodemus did not even know the concept of Salvation even after Jesus' explanations and one on one tutorial. "How can a man be born when he is old? Can he enter his mother's womb again and be born?" he asked Jesus in bewilderment. Jesus's explanations echoed the teaching of John the Baptist earlier quoted in **John 1:13.** Jesus mentioned water and Spirit as the catalysts of that change of life that takes place in Salvation. The Spirit, because it is the work of the supernatural. It is a spiritual occurrence done by Jesus in one's life. The water is the physical sign that the newly born again has identified himself or herself with fellow believers and has been not only washed in the water but symbolically "buried" with Christ and brought up again to life in Christ Jesus.

Jesus went on to distinguish between the two births: That which is born of the flesh is flesh, and that which is born of the Spirit is Spirit (John 3:6).

Jesus continued, expatiating further with the analogy of the wind, that everyone born of the Spirit (born again) is like the wind. He does not lead Himself or follow His own will or uncertain discretion, but led by the Holy Spirit:

Romans 8:14 compliments this scripture: *For as many as are led by the Spirit of God, they are the sons (children of God.)*

Are you a child of God? Yes, if you are born again. If you are not, just close this book or toss it on your bed or couch so you can seize this opportunity to accept the great gift of salvation. It is a gift and free of charge, as any gift should be. However, it cannot be given until it is wanted, desired, and received. If you are **only** baptized in water as a child or an adult, please know that you need to fulfill the spiritual aspect of it. It does not matter how long you have been serving in Church. It does not matter if you read your Bible or pray every day. It does not matter if you love people and people love you because you are nice, give to charities, and don't bother anybody. The scripture (Bible) cannot change:

> *Not by works of righteousness which*
> *We have done, but according to His*
> *Mercy, He saved us by the washing of regeneration*
> *and renewing of The Holy Ghost (Titus 3:5)*

You or anyone can say all you need is love because the Bible says love is the fulfillment of the law. They may quote the Bible more, that "Now abides faith, hope, love (charity), but the greatest of these is charity. True, love is the fulfillment of the law. But that is when you have been saved. The Bible says love covers multitudes of sin. Pardon me, and it is not talking or referring to the love of God covering our sins. It is referring to man to man's sin. It is referring to man's sin; whether it is offending our spouse, friend, siblings, church members, etc., love will forgive. Love, genuine love will let you forgive. Nothing, nothing in this world can be a substitute for salvation. Sin against God cannot be covered, and it must be washed away, cleansed. A person who is not born again is living in a state of sin. Even if he asks for forgiveness of the sin, what about uncountable others that he did not remember? Suppose he says, God, please forgive me all my sins. It does not work that way. The Bible states that we should not only **CONFESS**, but we must repent (have a change of heart of sin and then **FORSAKE** the sins.) The book of **Proverb 28:13** tells us that **anyone that covers his sin will not prosper (flourish), but whoever <u>confesses</u> and <u>forsakes</u> them shall have mercy**. Forsake means give up.

The Bible says the word of faith, which is the word of God preached by Jesus, and the apostles say:

That is thou (you) shall confess with thy (your) mouth the Lord Jesus, and shall believe in thine (your) heart that God hath (has) raised Him from the dead, thou (you) shall be saved. (Romans 10:9)

This is explained further by saying, "For with the heart man believeth (believes) unto righteousness; and with the mouth, confession is made unto Salvation. (Romans 10:10) To be a child of God and for God to be your father, you must be born again. That Jesus is not the son of God and that YOU cannot be a child of God is a lie, the greatest lie of all times. Some religion teaches that God has no son because He has no wife. That is human reasoning. True, God has no wife, but by the Spirit, He has a Son, called the only begotten of God the father. Jesus is the express image of God, the only-begotten. We that are born again are adopted by God. In John 1:14, the **"WORD" THAT WAS MADE FLESH IS** Jesus, whose glory is described as the glory of the only "begotten" of the father, full of Grace and truth. In Romans 8:15, all born again people have received the Spirit of "adoption" that makes us call God Abba (father).

CHAPTER TEN
THE CROSS REVISITED

In the year 2008, OCTOBER, my wife and I attended an international Christian conference called **SHAKE THE NATION CONFERENCE** in Baker, near Baton Rouge, Louisiana, where pastor (Dr) David Yonggi Cho of South Korea, Pastor of the largest Church in the World was the Chief, if not the sole guest speaker. We sat next to seats right behind him and his wife on the smallest Airplane I have ever flown on. That was our second plane from New York. My wife suggested that it was Pastor Yonggi Cho and wife we were sitting directly behind.

"No, it can't be him," I interjected with an air of finality. But she was right. We had boarded the same tiny plane as we all changed planes from a stopover. Soon we landed in Baton Rouge. The scene was a typical Hollywood red carpet reception outside the plane, with the glare of dazzling cameras snapping and filming. That's when I finally knew we had been on the same plane for a couple of hours.

The message centered on the concept of a cell church. The man of God taught how he grew such a large church of over 800,000 members through house cells known simply as **House fellowships** by many churches. What is the foundation of this large Church and the motive? Everything goes back to **THE CROSS**. The message of the cross is the bedrock of the gospel.

Many Churches today do not place due attention and emphasis on Salvation. Many are good with well-organized choir, great entertainment of Music and dancing, hype, dramatic preaching styles, and even organized outreach efforts but are not really making disciples of men. You go and fellowship in such Churches, and you will almost be preaching Salvation to some so-called elders. Members are dry, cold, and shallow in knowledge and understanding.

What is going on? Well, the foundation is shaky. It is not strong. Real salvation experience is missing. As a result, maturity is not attained. The result is a manifestation of all works of the flesh. All you see is the perfect picture of the Corinthian Church. Some mega-churches compromise their messages to avoid losing members; otherwise, they fear they will not be able to maintain their huge assets or is it their liabilities? The not-so-large Churches tend towards compromise so they can grow to be mega-churches. Go to such churches, and you will not hear a message or mention of sin, holy living, righteousness, consecration, crucifying of the flesh, and other core doctrines. Sure they will preach love. After all, you will not lose a member that way. Financial blessings and success will also come up regularly in sermons as it does not matter to them if the whole Church is carnal to the core.

In Dr. Yonggi Cho's Church, people have genuine experiences of Salvation, and they manifest Christ-like character in Church, at home, and in the marketplace. Employers would write and advertise vacancies in the Church so they could get honest, diligent, dedicated workers. That is how it should be in all churches. But if the message of the cross is not made fundamental, the experience of salvation will not be real even though a person could have been raised in a church. That person(s) might claim to be saved, though. One young, married lady said the same thing when I visited a branch of our Church in Nigeria. I was putting her through one-on-one deliverance. That was in 2018 during a two-week visit. The Spirit of God makes us to discern spirits and things if you have that gift. As I believe I have mentioned somewhere in this book, the Lord used to tell me by the Holy Spirit that so and so is not saved. Usually, I see the person first, with or without talking to the person, and the Lord says she is not saved. So I asked the young lady that she would need first to totally surrender and accept Christ in her life. She argued that she was in the choir, sometimes leading songs. I knew that. She said she grew up in the church since she was around 3 years old. I insisted I needed to lead her to Christ. She did not concur but submitted to my will because I am her pastor. I gave her 6 to 10 minutes to talk to God, confess her inadequacy, and accept Jesus. Then I started to minister deliverance by praying for her, commanding any contrary spirits to get out of her. I broke generational curses, and evil and unrighteous covenants she had made or was made on her behalf. After the first 15 minutes or thereabout, I asked that she open her eyes.

"What did you see if you saw anything?" I asked. "Yes, I saw a vision," she responded, "I saw a giant red cross."

"That is God confirming your new birth, and now you are saved." I lectured. She did not have to see any vision to confirm her Salvation. God just showed her a vision to confirm my assertion that she had not been truly born again. That means she knew the story of Jesus and many things about Jesus but never knew Jesus by relationship.

RELATIONSHIP

In the Christian faith, it is all about RELATIONSHIP. In other words, a relationship with Jesus is everything. It is impossible to have a relationship with God without knowing Jesus. It is like saying you know the Chairman of a corporation, the cars he owns, his office, and his name. All that information does not make you an employer of that corporation until you go through the director or CEO who will put you to work, and define your assignment and pay (salary). In other words, your functional relationship is with the one who is in-charge of the day-to-day operation of the corporation. And if you want to be employed, and go to the chairman, he will send you back to the director, who will determine where you fit in if you are employed. Your relationship builds up. So it is with coming to Jesus.

When you get saved, you have just experienced the cross. You are required to start carrying it. Jesus said anyone who will come after Him, let that person deny himself and take up his cross and follow Him. It is recorded by Matthew (16:24), Mark (8:34), and Luke (9:23).

Jesus was not talking about the symbolic physical cross - a big wooden cross or neck chain cross that many Catholics wear. The Bible is not against it. Some Angels of God wear a big golden cross. I have led two people to receive Jesus as their savior and Lord, who, while I was praying, saw a vision of the cross. I have just mentioned one of them earlier and the other, in New York, USA, who saw a chain around her neck with a dangling cross. The concern in carrying or wearing a cross is that the focus might be on that cross instead of the savior who died on it. There are many today who have turned the cross to be their God, their idol. They use it for fashion or carry it as an amulet.

What about the spiritual cross? Jesus used the metaphor of the cross to depict crucifying of the flesh. When you deny yourself, it will no longer be me, my will, my way, my life. When you carry or take up your cross, you are ready to uphold the gospel truth and to suffer if need be for the gospel of Jesus Christ. Your life will be one of total surrender so Jesus can be all in all. For me personally, it is not about me; nothing is about me. It is about Jesus. He is the priority and the center of my life. Everything about me revolves around Him. He called me into ministry. He is the one who determines that I do a pastoral Ministry of Salvation, healing, and deliverance. Tomorrow if He says, change to evangelistic ministry or prophetic ministry, no problem. He has the last say. Move to relocate to that city or to another, no argument, no excuse. You know why? It is because He is the Lord of my life, not just the Lord.

That should be the testimony of everyone who is born again and is taking up their cross and following Him. If Jesus is your savior and Lord, automatically, you are a son or daughter of God Almighty. When you know Jesus, you have known the Father God.

CHAPTER ELEVEN
REASONS WHY PEOPLE GET SAVED

Anyone that is born again will most likely fit in the list of reasons why people get saved. Here are some of the reasons.

When they hear the truth of the gospel (good news of salvation by the GRACE of God through the finished work of Christ on the cross), then their eyes are spiritually open, and they realize they had been ignorant and had been living in darkness.

When things of life and life itself become hard, it is like they have run into a dead-end of the road. They have tried everything, but nothing is working for them. What they need at that moment is not prayer but Jesus. God does not hear the prayer of sinners. In fact, the Bible says the prayers of a sinner are an abomination (a thing of disgust or hatred) to God. (proverb 28:9). Though God loves all people, but He is angry with the sinner every day (Psalm 7:11 and Psalm 5:5). He feels indignation with sinners every day. Yet, He loves them. How do we relate that together? One scripture says, "for God loves the world that He gave His only begotten Son, that whosoever believes in Him will not perish but have everlasting life (John 3:16). Another says God is angry with sinners every day. There is no ambiguity in each of the two scriptures, and there is no contradiction. It means simply that God loves the world, including sinners that God went as far as giving up His Son, Jesus Christ, to die for the world, so that the world might be saved, but because of the wicked ways of a sinner against God, He, God is angry, He is indignant. Does that not make sense? Yes, it does. You love your wayward son, but you are indignant of his ways. Suppose that son always drives while intoxicated. He comes to you asking for a new car. You most likely will deny him. You will ask that he quits drinking or he drives sober. By that, you are telling him that saving his life and the lives of other motorists and pedestrians are of much more value than a new car.

That is why God is not obligated to hear the prayers of a sinner. God will hear if the sinner is saying the sinner's prayer of repentance from his ways. God may hear if in a matter of life and death emergency. God may also hear sometimes to show His goodness and mercy.

Some people get saved when they are tired of sinful life. There is no testimony in wickedness, crime, and sinfulness. They want to live right and be accepted by society.

Some get saved when they are in trouble, like a pending court case or in big debt.

For some, it is when they are very ill or have a terminal illness. They ask for prayers on their sick or death bed. They usually don't refuse to accept Jesus and the gift of salvation at that point regardless of what their sickness will end up in.

When a person needs, God's protection from witchcraft attacks, they may run to God. A friend who became a Christian got born again, according to him, when his Father died in Nigeria. His Father, he said, was an Imam, a Muslim cleric. Suddenly he saw himself as an easy target of the enemies of his Father who used to protect him. If he became a Christian, he believed God would protect him from being killed supernaturally. He was right. It has been over.

40 years now, and nothing happened to him. He is a serious, committed Christian too.

Some get saved because their relatives or friends were praying for their salvation. They get convicted in their minds one day, and they surrender their lives to Jesus.

Some people of other religions have appearances whereby Jesus talked to them in a dream or in a trance, declaring that He is Jesus the only true way to salvation and to God. These people would not have believed, but they recount miraculous things or signs shown by Jesus that made them believe. This group is increasing daily because we are in the last days, and Jesus is showing mercy on hundreds of thousands of people. I have many stories of people who said they asked Jesus, "If you are real, show yourself to me; I really don't know what to believe."

Some gets saved when they realize hell is real, having read or heard about it.

The last group on my list are those who raise their hands up for salvation during altar calls in Church or outside or at a crusade ground. They say the sinner's prayer after the minister. Some of them know what they are saying and truly believe by faith.

For by grace ye (you) are saved through faith, and that not of yourself it is the gift of God, not of works lest any man should boast (Ephesians 2:8-9). However, many in this group are not truly saved. The probability is that they do not understand the narrative of what led the preacher or the evangelist to make an altar call. They just do not want to refuse blessings when the preacher says something like this. "Anyone who wants to give their life to Jesus, come here quickly so I can pray for you." People hardly pray more than saying the pattern of prayer that is wrongly called the Lord's prayer in **Matthew 6:9-13**. The Lord's prayer is actually in John Chapter 17. And in Matthew 26:36-46 in the garden of Gethsemane. As I said, people hardly take time to pray, but they love to be prayed for. So many people hearing a sermon respond to altar calls because they heard the preacher would pray for them. Often times you hear;

"If you want to give your life to Jesus, come to the altar." They probably do not even know what it means "to give your life to Jesus". What? Be a full-time preacher like you?

Some preachers do not even make altar calls. Often times you hear, "Raise up your hands where you are if you want to be born again." That is more understandable. Yet, they do not understand how the preacher gets there. Perhaps they even cannot say one sentence from his sermon or exhortation. They still raise up their hands anyway, especially when the preacher adds, "All eyes closed; everyone, please stay where you are. Just raise up your hand if you want to come to Jesus. I'm gonna pray for you now." Again, they raise up their hands. It is not because they believe or understand the phrase "come to Jesus." They see only the preacher and not Jesus, and not even angels are seen standing beside the preacher.

The truth is that some will not raise up hands or go to the altar as the case may be because they have no understanding of what they are required to commit to. In their hearts, some are saying: "I don't want to promise and don't do it. I'm not sure I will follow through." You see how we lose souls as ministers?

For those who signify by raising hands or who go to the altar to be prayed for, the minister or preacher truly tries to lead them to Jesus so they can be saved by using what I call an archaic and superficial method. Pardon me for calling it an archaic and superficial method. Maybe I should say a post-modern superficial method. The preacher goes like this:

"All of you raising up your hands, pray this prayer after me: I thank you, Jesus, for dying for me. I am sorry for my sins. Please forgive me and save my soul. Thank you for saving my soul." Then he adds, "if you just repeated that prayer after me, you have just been born again. Congratulations."

Many Christians and some ministers would ask, what is wrong with that prayer? It is what a sinner needs to be saved, they believe. True, some will be saved, and truly saved if these conditions are in place:

If they understood the message or explanations of their current life and what life in Christ is.

If they had been convicted of their old ways and have seen themselves in need of a new life in Christ.

If they already knew what it is to be saved, but they had not made up their minds in the past. They see now another opportunity or a last chance.

If any of these 3 conditions are present, the result will be genuine salvation or true salvation. Just like the Bible uses the adjective true, as in true holiness (Ephesians 4:24) and pure religion (James 1:27), true worshippers (John 4:23) and a true heart (Hebrews 10:22).

However, most people who raise their hands or walk to the altar during the altar call either soon forget they did that or did not know the meaning and implication. You will notice nothing new in their lifestyle as far as the Christian walk is concerned. Nothing changed, nothing remembered. Well, it is not their fault because the message of the cross was perhaps not presented to them in a simple, clear, understandable way. What then is essentially missing? Simplicity and thoroughness on the part of the evangelist or preacher.

Understanding and conviction on the part of the sinner. That is what is missing. Another essential that is missing is the lack of letting the unbeliever know who God is, and who Jesus and the Holy Spirit are.

CHAPTER TWELVE
SIN, SINNERS, AND DIVINITY

Before I go into the need to know who God is, let me briefly clarify a misconception about sin and sinners. You probably have heard someone being led to Jesus, or who you are witnessing to with tracts and Bible in your hands say something like, "we are all sinners.' He may even quote the passage of the Bible that says exactly that.

"All have sinned and come short of the glory of God." (Roman 3:23) The person you are preaching to about salvation is indirectly saying that you have no business judging me or accusing me of sin because, according to the Bible, we are all sinners, including you witnessing to me. To clarify that misconception, the Bible reference in Roman 3:23 says, "All have sinned ...." that is to say that each one of us "has sinned". The clause and even the entire sentence are in the past participle.

To put it another way, we can say that everyone had sinned in the past. The passage is not talking about present continuous tense or the third person singular present indicative form: Sins. If you or anyone ever sinned at one time in life, that sin remains and is qualified to be called a sinner for another 50 years and more. The person involved is called a sinner. Once the person is saved, he or she cannot be called a sinner any longer. His sin has been forgiven, and he is washed and cleansed by the shed blood of Jesus, which is the propitiation, the atonement for our sins.

If he is no longer a sinner, then the curse of coming short of the glory of God has been revoked. If he commits sin as a born-again person, he is not regarded as a sinner but as a believer who has sinned. You cannot lump him together with the person who has never been saved. One thing, though, is important. The sin must be repented of it is a willful sin, a premeditated sin. Once the Christian believer repents and departs from that sin, he is totally forgiven. He does not need to start all over and be born again, again.

The person who has never been born again is different. He is a sinner not because he once sinned but because he is living in that state of sin day in day out. He has not accepted and believed in Jesus as his savior and Lord. If he dies in that state of sin, the Bible says his soul will go to hell, a place of torment, darkness, and fire prepared originally for the Devil and his angels. Please let us get it right. Nobody is going to hell because he has sinned. He will go to hell because he has **NOT** accepted the only remedy of sin, Jesus, and His sacrificial death on the cross that took care of all our sins. Yes, Jesus paid that death penalty for all the sins of all people that are on earth and that will ever be born into the world. But if it is not accepted, that means it is rejected. There is no automatic, unconditional forgiveness and cleansing of sin. For a Christian who has just carelessly or mistakenly committed a sin, he or she must repent of that sin. He cannot claim that he has accepted the only remedy of sin, Jesus, and so does not need to repent. If he stubbornly refuses not to repent of that transgression, he might be chastised by God. If he is not chastised, he should repent quickly, or else his transgression can cause other transgressions and, in the end, plunge him into a state of backsliding. A Christian who dies in a state of backsliding or continues to commit sin is no better than an unbeliever. He keeps disobeying God. His relationship with God is marred. He is simply in rebellion. He is in danger of hell. Some all-knowing preachers, teachers or theologists may disagree, claiming that the backslidden person had once been saved and that he is forever saved and can in no way end up in hell. Only God knows how many thousands of souls they have deceived with this false doctrine. Jesus himself said clearly that *if your right eye offends you, pluck it out. It is better, more profitable for you if one of your members should perish than for your entire body to be cast into hell. Read it in Matthew 5:29- 30.*

THE WAGES OF SIN

One scripture says all have sinned as we referenced **Romans 3:23.** Let us look at another scripture:

"The wage of sin is death,
but the gift of God is eternal life through
Christ our Lord." (Romans 6:23)

If you stay put on Romans 3:23, that is if you get stuck on it, that all men have sinned and you think no matter what, we are all sinners, then you have to consider the other scripture just quoted about. **Romans 3:23** is talking, **Romans 6:23** is responding, and **Romans 10:9-10** is telling us exactly what to do in order not to receive the wages of spiritual and eternal death. Many people are spiritually dead. They do not believe in Jesus or in God that he sent His only begotten Son, (**John 3:16**.) Jesus says in **John 14:6**.

I am the way the truth and the life No one
comes to the Father (God) but by me.

There are four dynamics to this Scripture: Jesus is the way. Jesus is the truth. Jesus is the life. Nobody goes to God or has a relationship with God without going through Jesus. Believe it or not, that is the scriptural interpretation of it. It is not just what it implies. It is what it means.

By the grace of God and the power of the Holy Spirit, I have preached Jesus on the subway and elevated railroad Trains in Brooklyn, Queens, and New York City (Manhattan) for years, going or coming from work. I never held back on the truth that Jesus is the only way to God in this dispensation of grace from the church age to the present. That is, from Pentecost in the book of Acts of the Apostles to this day. On the trains, as we all know, are people of different faith and different religious persuasions. Jews, Moslems, Hinduists, Buddhists, Mormons, Catholics, Christians, and hosts of other religious people. All these believers in their faith would never agree, except Christians, that Jesus is the only way; in fact, some so-called Christians also believe that we're all serving the same God and can approach Him through different religions. No. Emphatic No. God does not accept this; it is the philosophy of man that God can be worshipped or approached (in prayer) through objects or through a man. That is idolatry.

DIVINITY

Jesus is the only one that is divine who came to the world to take the form of a man to redeem the world. There is no other way for God to come and live among men without incarnation. Suppose you or I see an angel in his glory. We will not be able to stand or look, how much more Jesus their master and Lord. So, He had to come in the form of man. Glory to God. Please read Philippians 2:5-11.

One of the most powerful scriptures that proves that we must confess and repent so we may escape damnation is our favorite one in Romans 3:23. "For all have sinned and come short of the glory of God."

WHO IS GOD?

I will state what I have stated before. One of the reasons some people who say the sinner's prayer after a minister remain the same, and no one sees any evidence or fruit of salvation in them is because they do not know who God is. They have not been prepared; their minds have not been prepared to know who God is.

The result is a mental ascent of "believe". To believe, you must have some faith. Not faith in faith or faith in yourself alone.

> *That if you confess with your mouth Jesus as Lord and believe in your heart that God raised Him from the dead, you will be saved. A person believes with the heart, resulting in righteousness, and with the mouth, he confesses, resulting in salvation (Roman 10:9-10). New American Standard.*

In the New American translation, it is the same requirement, though in a simpler diction. You must believe Him and also believe that Jesus rose up from the dead. This belief must be from the heart. Believe means to have a firm conviction, to accept as true, from your heart of heart. It is not a mental ascent or just a verbal utterance for the sake of utterance. When a person really believes, there will be no doubting. Such a person will be genuinely saved. He himself will know that he is saved. Right there, he will feel the love of Jesus in his heart, and he will never forget that day and that occasion. He may never remember the calendar date after some time, but he will remember that it is on a certain day of the week and in a certain place. Imagine if a person is asked, say, a visitor to a church. He is asked if he is born again. Imagine he starts to ramble, "I am not sure, well, I believe in Jesus, but I am not there yet; I got baptized when I was very young, like 3 years old."

Another one is asked if she has been saved. Imagine her saying, "I say the Lord's prayer before I go to bed, I pay my tithes to the church, and I read the psalms."

If you are a minister or a born-again believer who knows what you are doing, you will know right there that you need to minister to each of them and lead them to Christ. Both of them will most likely accept Jesus.

If we want people to be genuinely saved, we should let them know God and Jesus. Many know something about God that He is the maker of heaven and earth, but they do not know the part God played in salvation. They do not know the need to be saved. They may never have missed Church Sunday services and even maybe an usher in the Church. Yet salvation is missing. That is why we say things like a true child of God, genuine salvation, etc. Salvation is salvation. It is either you are saved, or you are not. But because we have "fake" everything, the Bible uses adjectives to qualify certain experiences. I have mentioned "pure" religion and "true" holiness - all in the Bible. Holiness is holiness. But because of falsehood and fakeness, the word true is used to distinguish true holiness from fake holiness.

PREPARATION

Preparing the mind of the persons to be led to accepting Jesus will make their experience unforgettable and real. They should be told how God created man and how the original sin came through the fall of man. God would not leave man and the world of sin like that forever. He therefore executed plan B whereby He would have to send God the Son to the world to redeem the world from sin and Satan. God the Son and God the Holy Spirit stayed in heaven while God sent God the Son. There is ONE God in THREE persons or personalities. He can manifest as God and can manifest as Jesus, or as the Holy Spirit, or as God the Father.

A colleague once told me how she was to teach Sunday school one Sunday at a church, the topic being TRINITY. She prayed to God asking how on earth she would be able to explain the TRINITY to the rest of the congregation. According to her, God talked to her in her dream that night, using the analogy of WATER. God said there is water. The same water can become an ice block. When heated, it can give off steam. If the steam is collected, water is formed.

All three have 3 distinct names and forms, yet it is water. The same is God, she was told.

CHAPTER THIRTEEN
THE ALMIGHTY JEHOVAH GOD

It is of utmost importance to ask, do you really believe there is God? I heard God speak to my heart to ask that question as I stood around the kitchen area. I did not know why, but I went quickly to my note and wrote the question down to avoid forgetting. Now I know why. If you or anyone does not really believe in God, he will not experience this saving grace for his salvation. Some at the point of making a decision for salvation, if asked who God is, he might say something like, oh, He is the man upstairs. I remember someone who said, I just know there is someone up there. He is not the man upstairs; He is the Living God. There is no other thing that men turned into "god" or called "god "that ever declared himself as a Living God. Those who worshiped other gods (idols) from the beginning of the world till today never claimed they worshiped a Living God. Their gods are dead. They might mold something or sculpture something like the figure of a man, with a nose, mouth, eyes. The fact is that they cannot see with their eyes or smell with their noses or deliver with their hands. God calls them dumb as those who fashion them are. Dumb (Psalm 115:3-8).

SELF PROCLAMATION

When Abraham was 90 years old, God appeared to him, declaring Himself: I am the almighty God; walk before me and be perfect. That is in **Genesis 17:1**, God is mightier than the mightiest men of old, greater than the greatest man that ever lived, stronger than the superman in any generation, older than the ancients of men, higher than the highest of peaks, richer than the richest billionaires combined and wiser than the wisest sage.

In ***Exodus 34:6-7,*** He made a proclamation of Himself to Moses as God came down from inside the cloud.

> *"And the Lord passed by before him, and proclaimed, the Lord God, merciful and gracious, longsuffering, and abundant in goodness and truth.*
> *Keeping mercy for thousands, forgiving iniquity and transgression and sin, and that will by no means clear the guilty; visiting the iniquity of the fathers upon the children and upon the children's children, unto the third and to the fourth generation."*

That was in the law. By the time you get to the prophets, something has changed, God never changed, but He can change circumstances, seasons, and situations; He is sovereign. In the book of Ezekiel Chapter 18, the Lord told prophet Ezekiel that there would be the end of a popular adage or proverb prevalent in Israel at that period of time:

> *"The fathers have eaten sour grapes, and the children's teeth are set on edge."*

In plain English, it means the parents have eaten sour grapes, and that caused the children to grind their teeth from the sour taste.

In other words, our fathers were the ones who sinned, and we, the children, are paying the penalty of their sins even though the fathers were punished already. This is an excuse for the younger generation. They did not admit their own sins but complained that they were just suffering because of their fathers' evil.

In Ezekiel Chapter 18, the Lord said that proverb would no longer be relevant because henceforth, whoever sins will bear the punishment alone. In verse 20 of that chapter 18, God said:

> *"the soul that sinneth (sins) it shall die."*

Remember, I have quoted the scripture in Romans 6:23 that says the wages (salary, paycheck) of sin is death. There are three forms of death – physical death, spiritual death, and eternal death.

Sin can cause physical death at any time. Even if the sinner lives to be a hundred years old, he cannot escape the spiritual and eternal death. Guaranteed. Spiritual death is the state of a person who has not been spiritually regenerated. He is in this world without Jesus Christ, without salvation. If he dies physically in that condition, his soul goes to a place of everlasting torment of dead endness. That is a dead-end for the soul and spirit of that person. No hope, no chance of repentance, no getting out. This is not my opinion. The Bible says the same thing several times, and Jesus started preaching it, then the apostles, then servants of God from Martin Luther, to John Bunyan, John Milton (paradise lost) John Wesley, down to Charles Finney, Sydney Elton, A.A Allen, John Lake, T.L. Osborn, Billy Graham, Oral Roberts, Reinhard Bonke, Morris Cerullo. Women, great evangelists like Aimee Semple, McPherson, Kathryn Khulman, and many, many contemporary others preached the same thing. Men of God like Enoch Adeboye, W.F. Kumuyi, Rodney Howard-Browne, Sunday Adelaja. Thank God they all preached repentance and salvation through faith in one and only: JESUS CHRIST.

That is what I preach too in the Church, here in the USA and in Nigeria and in Jamaica and to individuals outside of the Church, in Newspaper articles, on Social media. That is what I will preach to the end of my life here on earth, either by death or by rapture.

JESUS CHRIST THE SAVIOR

It is also of paramount importance for an unbeliever coming to Christ or being led to Christ to know something about the Jesus you want them to believe. People have grown up or been taught that Jesus is just a prophet or a man who founded the Christian faith, or an ordinary man like everybody, but very nice, gentle, and innocent, who went about preaching and unfortunately met His death in the hands of the authority. Is that all? Will that make an unbeliever want to believe and come to that Jesus, who the unbelievers believe could not save Himself from the death on the cross? We should do ourselves a favor and the people we want to lead to Christ by letting them know the basic things, like who is

Jesus and what did He do? Why do they and all people need Him? We cannot explain God or Jesus, and God is infinite. Same with Jesus and the Holy Spirit. When we mention the word "God", we may be referring to all trio (trinity) or God the Father.

When God the Father talked in Genesis 1:26: ***"He said, let us make man in our own image, after our likeness."***

He used the plural form of "me" and "my," so when God in Genesis 1:1 created heaven and earth, it was these three, Jehovah Adonai, Jesus Christ, and Holy Spirit that created heaven and the earth. This truth is echoed in the New Testament book of John 1:1-15. Jesus is that "WORD' who was with God and was God. All things were made by that word (co-creator), and in Him was life and that life is the light of men. Interesting scripture. So, you see, Jesus was at the beginning of the creation of all things. When He was ready to come to the world to redeem us, He had to leave His glory and imperial majesty to be born by a woman through Holy Spirit conception. The God who put the seed of baby in us humans was able to put the spiritual seed of pregnancy in the Virgin Mary. Every process had to be holy and pure.

WHAT GOD SAID

In Isaiah, one of the major prophets of the Old Testament, God spoke to him in a vision that a child would be born. His name shall be called, according to Isaiah 9:6 wonderful, counselor, the Mighty God, the Everlasting Father, the Prince of Peace.

In the book of Matthew 17, the same God who gave the prophet Isaiah the revelation and the names of Jesus mentioned above also made a declaration of Jesus. The scene was on a high mountain where Jesus had taken Peter, James, and John. There, Jesus was transfigured before these three apostles. The Bible says Jesus' face did shine as the sun and His raiment (clothe) was white as snow. Right there appeared with them, Moses and Elijah. When Peter saw the two old testament prophets appear with them, he (Peter) said to Jesus that it would be good to make three tabernacles, one for Jesus, one for Moses, and one for Elijah. As he was saying this, a bright cloud overshadowed them, and a voice out of the cloud boomed: (Matthew 17:6)

> *"This is my beloved Son,*
> *in Whom I am well pleased; hear ye Him."*

That was God the Father accentuating the deity of Jesus. Moses and Elijah are not anywhere to be grouped with Jesus. He is their Lord. Peter needed to be corrected, and the world needed to know that Jesus is the only begotten Son of God and the express image of His (God's) personality and deity, who cannot even be grouped with the angels of God because the Bible in Hebrews 1:3-8 speaks of Him sitting on the right hand of the majestic throne of God on His (Jesus) own throne in the heavens of heaven. He is much placed better than the angels by inheritance and by His more excellent name. In the passage named above, the book of Hebrew asks a rhetorical question: To which of the angels did God say at any time, "You are my son, this day I have begotten You?" In fact, we are told further in the passage of the scripture that when God brought forth Jesus into the world through the Virgin Mary, God commanded: Let all the angels of God worship Him.

CAN DEMONS TELL THE TRUTH?

Some people cannot just tell the truth. Jesus once rebuked the Pharisees, who He said were like their Father, Satan, who He described as the Father of lies. But, at least for once, Satan's angels, the demons, told the truth. In Mark Chapter 5, Jesus went to the Eastern shore of the Sea of Galilee in a location called Gadara, where a demon-possessed man met Him. The miserable man ran to Jesus to worship Him. His body and soul had been taken over by a legion (at least 2,000) of demons. But the man's spirit worshipped Jesus. The demon head (leader) cried out:

"And cried with a loud voice, and said, what have I to do with You Jesus, You Son of the highest God? I adjure You by God that You torment me not." **Mark 5:7**

You have not misheard or misread. Demons (evil spirits) as supernatural being know Jesus, and if you are born again, they know you too.

When in 2009, a young lady of 17 years of age was brought to me for deliverance during a visit to Nigeria, I had a hard time trying to lead her to Jesus. She did not want to confess her sins to God and accept Jesus into her life. Not even when I painted the picture and reality of hell as a consequence for unrepentant sinners' punishment - witches, thieves, liars, murderers, fornicators, adulterers, etc.

She did not deny she was a witch who, with her cohorts, killed people by supernatural means, draining them of their blood and eating their flesh. She confessed to me when I asked but would not repent and forsake her evil ways. After a while, she said she would be killed by her cohorts because of the blood oath of loyalty they all swore to. I asked her who she thought I was, "A servant of God. "she responded. "How do you know that because I never introduced myself in any way?"

"I know because I see a cross on your forehead," she said with an air of certainty. I said she was right and that if she got born again, there would be a mark on her too, a light or a cross, and no witch would be able to kill her because of God's divine mark of protection.

That minute, I mean the moment I said that, you could see her countenance changed. She gave her consent to come to Jesus. Thanks to God, she was led to Christ.

It makes it easier, and I will say valid if the person you are leading into repentance and acceptance of the free salvation really knows who God is and who Jesus is.

> *"For whosoever shall call upon the name of the Lord shall be saved. How then shall they call on him whom they have not believed? And how shall they believe in him of whom they have not heard? And how shall they hear without a preacher?"*
> *(Romans 10:13-14)*

CHAPTER FOURTEEN
WHAT JESUS DID FOR THE WORLD

Not only is it necessary to let the person or people you are trying to lead to Jesus know who Jesus really is, but what He did for this person and the whole of humanity. It should be presented in a clear, simple, and understandable way, something like this: Jesus in heaven in the TRINITY (one God in 3 unique personalities) left His unapproachable majestic glory to come briefly to the world to redeem the world from sin, death, and destruction. There was a need that someone, not two, must die as a scapegoat for the sins of the whole world. And this death must be by shedding of His blood.

To remind you again, there can be no redemption without the shedding of blood (Hebrews 9:22). To redeem means to ransom, to free or rescue by paying the price to be free from the consequences of sin.

God the Father loved mankind so much that He sent Jesus to do the redemptive job. Knowing there was no one else qualified to do it, Jesus accepted to come and execute the task. If He did not accept it, the whole of humanity would have been doomed - unable to be cleansed of sin, unable to be rid of death, and unable to possess eternal life. We should daily be grateful to God and to Jesus for their great, mightily great love. The most powerful scripture that captured the great sacrifice of Jesus, leading to the redemption of man, is the one that is most quoted by sinners and saints alike

For God so loved the world that He gave
His only begotten Son that whosoever believes
On Him should not perish but have Everlasting life
(John 3:16)

MAN'S ONLY HOPE

The scripture in John 3:16 just told us what the only hope of man is: salvation. That is not all. This salvation is by Jesus and Jesus only. That is not all. Everyone is covered under this blood covenant. That is not all. It is not automatic coverage. It is consent coverage. You must consent to it by believing in Jesus and His finished work on the cross. It is then your eternal life in heaven and in the New World to be created will be yours.

"Believe" is to have a firm conviction about something, to accept it as true, to feel sure of the truth of. This kind of belief is of the heart, as stated in Romans 10, that man believes unto righteousness with the heart. The preceding verse, **Romans 10:9, states:**

> *"That if thou (you) shall confess with thy(your) mouth the Lord Jesus and Shall believe in thine (your) heart that God hath raised Him from the dead, thou shall be saved."*

You see, everything in Christendom is by faith, which means belief. When anyone truly believes in their heart, the person(s) shall be truly saved. That is grace. No rituals, no work. Just believe. That is grace.

Again, let me reiterate that going by the recommendation in the preceding pages ensures a more viable result. It guarantees success more than just asking an unbeliever say the sinner's prayer or to raise hands, signifying they want to be saved. My recommendation to anyone who wants to lead a person or people to Christ is to briefly let them know God as the creator (Maker) of heaven and earth and all things in them. It should be emphasized that this God is eternal, invisible Godhead, existing and manifesting as a Triune God - the Father, the Son, the Holy Ghost. They, as one God, are omnipotent (able to do all things), omniscient (all-knowing), and omnipresent (all-seeing). He is believed by faith, not by proof. He is above scientific search. Our finite mind is too small to comprehend the infinite God who has no beginning and no end. Dogs and cats live with man. They can never be trained to learn safe and successful cooking or learn to fly an Aircraft. It is too complex for their limited intellect. So is God to us.

Then we should let them who are to be saved know Jesus - who He is, why He had to come to the world to be born incarnate, and the truth about Him being the only way of Salvation. It gets more personal when we let them know that Jesus died for "you", whoever they or that person is, and that "you" only have to make the decision to accept Christ and the finished work on the cross. The person(s) who just made that decision based on the above explanations will no doubt know what they are into and will tend to be serious and careful with their new faith and love the Lord, who is now their Savior and LORD. As Lord, they will not find it hard to obey Him. Everything will just fall into place, including the constant urge to want to know more about their Lord by reading and studying the Bible and also wanting to have a healthy relationship with Him by combining it with prayer. We, believers, pray to God in the name of Jesus.

It is high time you took that great decision and get saved now. Tomorrow might be too late. Heaven and hell are before everyone. There is no other place. It is your choice.

CHAPTER FIFTEEN
WHAT TO DO AFTER SALVATION

1. **Stay away from sin.** *(Psalm 4:4, 1 John 3:8-10)*

New believers should know that to do everything possible to avoid sin is no brainer, to use a common parlance. Galatians 5:1 says, "It is for freedom that Christ has set us free. Stand firm, then, and do not let yourselves be burdened again by a yoke of slavery" (new international).

Do not be deceived by the lies of men from the devil that it does not matter what we do as believers, that no matter what, God loves us, and no one can snatch us away from Him. True, God loves us. It is also true that no one can snatch us from Christ, that is only true as long as we abide in Jesus and keep our ourselves (1 John 5:18) But look at these scriptures:

> *"Ye adulterers and adulteresses, know ye not that the friendship of the world is enmity with God? Whosoever, therefore, will be a friend of the world is the enemy of God" (James 4:4)*
> *"Love not the world, neither the things that are in the world. If any man loves the world, the love of the father is not in him. For all that is in the world, the lust of the flesh, the eyes, and the pride of life is not of the father but of the world. And the world passeth away and the lust thereof, but he that doeth (does) the will of God abideth forever" (1 john 2:15-17) king James Version.*

Yes, God loves us, but if we do whatever we like, living in sin after Salvation, loving the worldly things of godlessness, making money our priority pursuit, being arrogant, and lusting after sinful things, then we are enemies of God as that passage quoted above says. Does God love His enemies? The Bible says, let God arise and let His enemies be scattered, let them also that hate Him flee before Him (Psalm 68)

Does God love sinners? You bet. But not the kind of love that will make sinners, unrepented sinners, go to heaven. If God's love for all sinners covers all sinfulness and all wickedness, then no sinner will be in Hell now, in the past, and in the future.

Take for instance, an armed person robbing a bank, he shot one or two persons not fully complying with his orders. The cops stormed the place, and he was shot dead. Is he going to heaven? If you say 'No,' you are not judging. You are just being factual. Otherwise, heaven now will be full of murderers, pedophiles, kidnappers of children, and terrorists. By God's grace, we know the Bible by the spirit of understanding, through teachings and writings of true men of God called to ministry, and through seminary Bible college education. You don't have to go to Bible college to know sound doctrine, but you have to be in a bible preaching, Bible Teaching church, sit under committed and gifted teachers, and read/study on your own daily. That is what the early Christians in the book of Acts did, and they grew to be evangelists, teachers, and prophets. God's love for sinners is centered on their repenting of sins and getting saved. God loves so much that if a sinner turns to Him in penitence, He, God, will forgive and save such a person. That is love. When a person is saved, that person should know that old things have passed away and all things about him have become new because he is a new creature. That is from the scripture we have already explained in this book. Also, Romans 6:1-3 asks three questions in a roll:

> *"What shall we say then? Shall we continue in sin that grace may abound? God forbid How shall we, that are dead to sin, live any longer therein? Know ye not that so many of us that were baptized into Jesus Christ were baptized into His death?"*

2. **As a new Christian is to find a Bible-believing, Bible-preaching church to be a member of; pray that God leads you.** Do not just visit occasionally. Be a member. Find out the schedule of services and be there on time consistently. The Church does not have to be the nearest to your residence. Watch in case a friend or neighbor invites you to his or her Church. Go, but watch out for the way and manner of their service(s). Beware of where they use strange objects like candles, incense burning, water mixed with other things, or water by itself. The only acceptable New Testament object is olive oil. Other religious paraphernalia must be avoided. They could be objects of rituals and occult. Flee such a place.

3. **Get a good "study Bible" or two, and study it with your own study plan.** You may start reading book by book, starting from Genesis, or just follow a devotional book. As you read and study daily, combining it with the church Bible study on weekdays and Sunday teachings or Saturdays as the case maybe you will be amazed how quickly your knowledge of the Bible will grow even if you have never been in Church all your life.

4. **Find in Church, information about water baptism.** It usually takes a process; you might be put in disciple class or baptismal class.

5. **Prayer is an essential part of the Christian life. Start praying as soon as you get saved.** Let prayer be a daily regimen. Morning prayer is the best, as early as you can wake up. This practice will give you an edge over the busy activities of the day. You can start with 15 minutes of prayer and about 10 minutes of Bible reading. Then you can do more in the evening before hitting the bed. By the time you know it, you will be praying one hour. I mean one hour of Bible and praying. That is how we grow. As a new believer in those days, I used to devote at least one hour to worship, prayer and Bible. Within months, I used to spend 2 hours. Having developed myself over the years, it was not hard for me to go 3 hours. Whenever I traveled out of town to one favorite prayer ground, I would spend two days. With no

disturbance or hindrance, I would just be in the presence of God for 6 hours at a time. Sometimes it is 3 hours at a time and another 3 hours later. One day I was in His presence praying from 9 am to 9 pm, 12 hours nonstop. The more you pray, the more grace you have to pray and the more you love prayer. You just want to be in the presence of your heavenly father. That is love. In the same vein, God wants you to be in His presence - even more than you want to be in His presence. He loves you more than you can ever love Him.

Bible is our food, our daily spiritual food. Prayer is our exercise. A normal, healthy person anywhere is the one who eats daily and exercises regularly. If he does not eat at least two square meals a day, he will go malnourished, ending up developing some ailments. Suppose he does not go to the gym or does not exercise at home regularly (even if it is just a brisk walk or jugging). In that case, he will have problems with his muscle, blood circulation, heart functioning, constipation, digestion, and even life-threatening diseases. If he does not eat and exercise at all, he will, of course, die. It is the same in the spiritual world. A Christian who does not read the Bible will soon backslide because he is not fed spiritually. The Bible is our guide and instruction manual (2 Timothy 3: 16). From backsliding (drawing back), he may totally abandon the faith, only now to say, "God is in my heart. I believe there is God." Check that person out, and he is back to his old ways. The dog returns to its own vomit (Proverb 26:11 and Peter 2:22). In the same vein, if he does not pray no more, he will be entering temptation upon temptation. "Watch and pray," Lord Jesus says, "so that you will not enter into temptation." (Matthew 26:41). The state of spiritual death is when a person has no fellowship or relationship with God. It is the same state if he totally abandons the faith.

6. **Search your house for any physical, symbolic idol in the form of a statue, image, religious artifacts or materials, colored candles, incense, spiritual bracelets, strange rings, strange religious or witchcraft practice books, magic practice books, oils, etc.** A small or sizeable cross bought in a Christian

bookstore and olive oil bought at a regular grocery store are not objects of idolatry, provided you don't see them as objects of your trust. You should not idolize them. The best thing is to be on the safe side. Bible, biblical literature (books like this one), and olive oil for anointing yourself, your family members when sick, and any other thing you want to anoint at home is okay. Any of those things I have listed in the beginning of number 6 should be discarded and trashed or burned. Do not give it to people. Many things are pure demonic objects that invite the presence of demons to that house or the person that owns them. It is tantamount to giving permission for the demons to come. Any servant of God who knows something about deliverance knows this fact. Even in the Bible, new believers in Jesus Christ took all those artifacts to the apostles to be burned.

> *"And many that believed came, and confessed, and showed their deeds. Many of them also which used curious arts brought their books together and burned them before all men, and they counted the price of them and found it fifty thousand pieces of silver." (Acts19:18-19)*
> *Please read also Acts 17:29-32*
> *and 2 Samuel 5:19-21.*

7. **The last thing to know and do after Salvation is to witness Christ Jesus with your testimony of who you were before and how Jesus has saved you from condemnation to salvation, from darkness onto His marvelous light and from the brink of hell and eternal torment to the gate of heaven and eternal life.** Let them know that you are now reconciled with God and that it is now committed onto you to have others reconcile to Him.

> *"And all things are of God who hath (had) reconciled us to Himself by Jesus Christ, and hath (has) given to us the ministry of reconciliation; To wit (that*

> *is to say) that God was in Christ, reconciling the world unto Himself, not imputing their trespasses (sin) unto them; and hath committed unto us the word of reconciliation." (2 Corinthians 5:18-19)*

In the following verse (20), the Bible says we are **AMBASSADORS for CHRIST**.

Yes, you and I are ambassadors representing Christ here on earth. What a great and lofty status. It is greater than being an ambassador of the Queen or King of the United Kingdom to America or the American ambassador to France or to any nation. You are representing the king of kings and the Lord of Lords.

Witness to someone or two that you are getting a service from. (Mechanic, Dry cleaner, Uber, Lyft drivers), or a person you are buying from (store owner, car dealer or salesperson), or someone or two at a supermarket. Check in Google and send for TRACTS literature that you can hand out to people you witness to. It makes my job easier when I witness with TRACTS which they can read when they get a chance. It is also good for those who have no time to hear you. If they do, you can spend from one minute to five minutes, depending. There were times I was giving out new Bibles as I witnessed in the trains and on the subway platforms. You can also try if you can invest some money in the Bible once or twice a year. You can also get more copies of this book to give to friends and co-workers. With my prayers and yours, they will be saved in Jesus' Holy name.

Remember that the Christian faith is not a religion. It is a relationship. God is not a dictator commanding us to do this, do that, do not do this, or that. He wants a relationship as a loving father to His children.

Remember that there is only ONE WAY to heaven: Jesus.

> *"I am the way, the truth, and the life;*
> *No man comes to the father but by me." (John 14:6.)*

Jesus made this self-declaration, an answer to what all the world has been searching for – TRUTH, LIFE, and the WAY to worship God. There is no or ever was any head of a religion or faith that has ever declared that he is the truth or the life. The most they say is that they have found the truth. They fail to state eloquently, logically, and clearly what that truth is and how it can liberate mankind. The result is confusion and human religious' philosophy - like Buddha, whose full name is Siddhartha Gautama. The founder of Buddhism admitted on his death bed that he was still searching for the truth.

Jesus did not just say He knew the truth of what life is or the way to get to God. He said He is the TRUTH the whole world has been searching for, and the WAY and LIFE itself - what a true self-declaration.

Remember, the Christian life is that of growth. Like a typical biological child, a newly born-again person starts growing from day one.

> *"As ye have therefore received Christ Jesus the Lord, so walk ye in Him. Rooted and built up in Him, and established in the faith, as ye have been taught, abounding therein with thanksgiving; beware lest any man spoil (destroy) you through philosophy and vain deceit, after the tradition of men, after the rudiments (principles) of the world, and not after Christ." (Colossians 2:6-8) JESUS!*
> *That is all you need.*

CHAPTER SIXTEEN
FORGIVENESS IS NOT WHAT YOU THINK IT IS

Forgiveness is so important that I have saved it for one of the last chapters. It is absolutely essential - from day ONE of your salvation to your last breath on earth. In the pattern of prayer that Jesus taught us in **Matthew 6:9-15**, He emphatically warned that if you do not forgive men, your heavenly Father (God) will also not forgive you your sins. If you dream or God tells you or make you see a dead relative or friend in hell, they were not saved before they died. If they were once saved, then it is because they had abandoned God and the faith, and were living in sin and disobedience, unrepentant. But if they were vibrant Christians before they died, they most likely did not forgive someone. Forgiveness must be from the heart. It is not what you just simply say with your mouth. You have to let it go completely. Here you must be wise and knowledgeable. If someone close to you has offended you greatly, do not just say, I forgive and then cut off communication with that person. You should go and resolve it in person or over the phone, avoiding any argument. Remember, you want to forgive, not to justify yourself or maintain your innocence. Tell the person to forgive you if you had offended, and you as a child of God want to forgive as well. If they raise an argument, just maintain your position that you just want peace. If he does not cooperate or listen, go to him with another person if you are all in the same Church. If not, still try to go with another person he knows. If he would not listen, just let him know you are not holding a grudge and that you have forgiven. You don't have to force back friendship and relationship, but you should remember that you can win him back or lead him to Jesus by your gentleness and love. Always try to be on talking terms with all people. There is nothing like "we don't talk to each other" in Christianity. Be wise and be loving as your heavenly father.

SOME LIKELY DIFFICULT QUESTIONS NEW BELIEVERS ASK.

1. If Jesus is the only way to God, how about those who never heard about Jesus?

ANSWER

Those who never heard about Jesus will be judged by their hearts, by the work of the law written in their hearts by God. This is their conscience. They will be judged by their thoughts and their conscience and the kindly work these two elements have produced. Read Romans 2:11-16

2. Are Catholics Christians?

ANSWER

If you ask them if they are Christians, they will say, "I am Catholic." I have heard that countless times, nevertheless, whoever is born again, having Jesus as savior and Lord, and work righteousness is acceptable to God regardless of their denomination. However, any church or denomination that does not follow the apostles' doctrines as we see it played out in the book of Acts of the Apostles cannot be called a Christian Church. The apostles' doctrines are Christ's doctrines; they called the disciples Christians (after Christ) first in Antioch and then other places.

While we have born again believers in all true churches, anyone or any church that worships any being or deity other than God (Father, Son, and the Holy Ghost) only is not a living church. Bowing to or worshipping an image or statue of any being or deity is pure idolatry. Any church or person that prays to God in the name of any being, Saint, or deity other than Jesus is practicing idolatry or idol worship. We are commanded not to do that in Exodus 20. It is Jesus, all about Jesus, not His mother or earthly father or any living or departed saint. From the Old Testament to all of the New Testament, it is all about Jesus. Jesus challenged the Jews to search all the scriptures, which they admitted, it shows them that they have eternal life. But it is the same scriptures that testify of Jesus, He told them.

J.C. Loberters captured it all:

> *"The Old Testaments cries:*
> *Behold, He comes!*
> *The gospel: Behold, He dies!*
> *The Acts of the apostles: Behold, He lives!*
> *The epistles shouted: Behold, He saves!*
> *And the apocalypse (Revelation), with Hallelujah*
> *clause: Behold, He reigns!*

3. How often do I need to fast as a Christian?

ANSWER

Fasting and prayer are essential in our Christian Journey. Prayer is your two-way vertical communication with God. It is your telephone conversation with heaven. If you will listen, God talked to us during or after prayer. You will need to develop the skill of hearing the voice of God. Fasting is relevant if you are committed to having a long time with God in prayer, say a whole day or hours. If your prayer duration is 1 hour a day, you can still fast, perhaps once a week. It will help in developing your ability to last longer in the future. Fasting will also help you put the flesh (the natural tendency to sin) in subjection. It is advisable to fast when you are praying over a serious or tough situation. It makes you focus on that issue. It saves you precious time that could have been wasted cooking, washing, and eating. If you choose to fast anytime, you must pray. Fasting without time to pray is an exercise in futility. It is starvation or just trying to shed some weight.

4. When I fast, should I skip meals or just a meal?

ANSWER

Fasting means abstinence from food. Some Christians skip two meals and eat just a meal, dinner especially. The dinner is usually eaten any time after 6 pm. Some break their fast at 5 pm. For those who have the grace, they don't eat the whole day, they just drink water. Even when breaking at 6 pm, you can still drink water in the course of the day, depending on your health. Some go for 3 days with only water. Some have developed themselves to do 7 days. If in the future you start on 3 days or 7 days, make sure you are home, away from work and stress. The more we fast and pray, the more power there is to preach, heal the sick and deliver the oppressed and the possessed in the name of Jesus Christ.

5. How do I know it is God talking to me and not the voice of the Devil?

ANSWER

True, the devil talks and can talk to a Christian. However, it is so easy to distinguish one from the other. When you hear the silent voice of God in your spirit, check it out if it does not contradict the Bible, the word of God. If it does, do not even pray about it; just jettison it. The voice of the Devil will always tell you or lead you to sin. For instance, if you hear that you should get yourself a Rolls Royce car, your money is for Toyota Camry or Lexus. Think about the monthly payment; think about the down payment without going all over to borrow money. The devil probably wants to feed on your ego. That is the sin of pride. In the same vein, if you are married, you hear a voice saying divorce, divorce. God will never tell you to divorce. Even in the case of adultery with your spouse, God will never say go and divorce. He will leave the option to you. Also, you have the option to forgive, except your spouse does not even want to continue in the relationship.

The best thing and the best remedy against hearing satan's voice is to make your heart right and your thoughts pure. When your mind is occupied with evil carnal things you have fed yourself with on the internet, television, useless worldly sensual magazines, your thoughts will be clogged with impurity. Satan will have his field day. By the grace of God, I do not hear from the devil because he knows I will instantly discern him. So he does not bother to talk to me. If he tries to bring an impure thought, I will knock it down instantly. So, in voice and in dreams, it is God talking to me. When you let the word of God occupy your mind with singing in your spirit or loudly, with meditation (thinking and reviewing) on the word of God and the greatness and goodness of God, your heart will be right and your thoughts pure. Before you know it, God will be giving you wonderful dreams and revelations. As you continue consistently (not today up, tomorrow down roller coastal Christian life), God will be bringing the Bible alive to you with much understanding of the mystery of His Kingdom. Jesus will be showing, Himself in dreams, talking to you, and even taking you on trips to heaven in your dreams. These things are evident in my life, glory to God. He, without fail, has been giving me the direction of my life. He stopped me from pursuing a law degree after my first degree in English. He told me the exact date to start a church which I now pastor, and told someone else, a minster of God, to tell me the name of the ministry. God has told me two times to move to Queens, New York, and ten years later to Long Island, New York. Friend, there is nothing like having a relationship with the Lord. Before I became a pastor, I had prayed for people and fellow Christians, and the Lord had healed cancer of the breast, cleaned out strange skin disease on four members of a family, healed a young woman with 8 years of full-blown AIDS when in the early 1990s there was no cure for AIDS, healed two of my own children with prayers only, one of them at 2 years old who would not eat or drink anything for days and looked like a skeleton.

This is to encourage my readers, newly saved or veteran Christians alike. You love the Lord totally and unreservedly as your number one, your priority, your total trust, and love being in His presence; instead of spending hours and hours in front of the television and social media, He will move for you and show Himself to you. Do you know you can see God Almighty Himself? Though He will not let you see His face.

6. What are tithes, and should I give them in Church?

ANSWER

Without delving into the scriptures and overwhelming you, I will say it is good to give to the Lord to upkeep and maintain the Church. Tithes started in the book of Genesis, not just in the book of Malachi Chapter 10. Those who oppose tithing in Church, what have they prescribed as an alternative? The Church, especially in developed countries like America are made comfortable for worshippers – heating, air conditioning, carpeting, sitting, the printing of program literature, giving to those in dire need and temporarily out of work in Church, running the church bus, and giving salary or allowance to the pastor or Bishop. They work full-time in the Church or ministry. In the Church I briefly attended for about four years, when I was 8, 9, 10 or 11 years old in Nigeria, they gave more than tithes (ten percent of income). Whenever they needed something, people in the Church would be going to the altar area to drop money. A large piano was bought, for instance, in just one giving. Someone or a couple of worshippers might even pay for a particular expense. Tithes, to me, are the cheapest we can give to God. When a church needs to purchase a building, members need to donate maybe a couple of thousands of dollars each... Not only should we give thousands of dollars in such cases, but we should also individually give to less privileged brethren and those around us, (neighbors) who have needs. This is what our God wants us to do throughout the Bible.

7. Heaven and hell – are they real, can a Christian go to hell?

ANSWER

Yes, heaven is real, and hell is real. We need to read and study the Bible and sit under teachings in Church so that we can be well versed in the word of God. A Christian cannot go to hell if the Christian lives a Christ-like life of righteousness and obedience to the word of God. If however, according to Galatians 5:18-24, the Christian lives a careless life of non-submission to the spirit of God. In other words, if they live in the flesh, he will have no choice but to fulfill the carnal works of the flesh. These works of the flesh in verses 19 and 20 of Galatians 5, or part of these works will manifest. Fornication, hatred, violent anger, heresies, drunkenness, to mention a few, will be found in his life, perhaps he went back to his old ways, or he never renounced them totally after giving his life to Jesus. Verse 21b of the same scripture says, "They which do such things shall not inherit the kingdom of God," And that is if they fail to repent and forsake them. Bible experts tell us that the word SHEOL is translated 31 times as hell and also 31 times as the grave. In the New Testament, Jesus made allusions to hell as a place where there is torment and ever-burning fire, as discussed fully in the early chapters of this book. See mark 9:43 – 48 and Luke 16:19 – 31.

8. WHO IS THE HOLY SPIRIT?

ANSWER

You should not have forgotten that I mentioned the mystery of the TRINITY a couple of times, that is, ONE God in THREE separate and distinct personalities. The Holy Spirit or Holy Ghost is the third person of the Trinity. He is real, just as Father God and the Son, Jesus are real. They are spirits with spiritual bodies. When Jesus was about to leave this world, He told His disciples that another comforter like Him would be sent by the father, in the person of the Holy Ghost. Jesus called the Holy Spirit comforter and teacher. As Jesus revealed, the Holy Ghost came to the world on the day of Pentecost in Acts chapter 2.

When a person gets saved, the Holy Spirit that convicts all men and women, and leads them to be converted (saved) enters into them in a measure. When Jesus baptizes the person with the Holy Spirit, then a full measure of Him (Holy Spirit) dwells in that person.

The Holy Spirit is the spirit behind the power of God, signs, wonder, and miracles. He is on earth with us and in us. We should be aware that the Holy Spirit is in us, and we should not grieve Him with uncontrolled emotions of anger, dirty talks, and evil thoughts.

If grieved, He will leave that moment. He is gentle, loving, but sensitive.

I know you must have been saved by reading this book because I trust the Holy Spirit's power of conviction. But if you still have not made a decision, now is the time to make it. It is a decision of life – the greatest decision any human being can ever make is the decision to repent, forsake old ways and invite Jesus to save his or her soul. If you believe in Him and that He will save you, He will surely save.

There is no one so bad he cannot be saved, and no one so good he needs not be saved.

9. What is the gospel that we Christians have to share with people?

ANSWER

Gospel is the good news or the good message of salvation and the life, death, resurrection, ascension, and return of our Lord Jesus Christ.

10. What is rapture of the Church?

ANSWER

Actually, it should be called the rapture of the BRIDE OF JESUS. Rapture is the catching away of all saved souls in the world in the twinkling of an eye, when we will meet the Lord up above in the clouds beyond the cloud. Simply, we will be caught up to heaven, where the marriage supper of the Lamb (Jesus) with us will take place. It is the ultimate reunion called marriage. It is not all church members but all who are saved that will be raptured. That is why the scripture in Titus 2:11 says that ***"For the grace of God that brings salvation has appeared to all men, teaching us that denying ungodliness and worldly lusts, we should live soberly, righteously, and godly in this present world, looking for that blessed hope and the glorious appearing of the great God and our savior Jesus Christ."***

In Thessalonians 5:1-6, Apostle Paul stated the need for us to be ready for this momentous event because it is very close, closer than when he wrote it some two thousand one hundred and fifty years ago. He also wrote in the preceding chapter 4:13-17 what exactly rapture is. Before Paul's epistle, the Angel told the Apostles when Jesus was being taken up to heaven after an appearance to His disciples after His resurrection.

> **"And while they looked steadfastly toward heaven as He went up, behold, two men stood by them in white apparel, which also said "ye men of Galilee, why stand ye gazing up unto heaven? This same Jesus, which is taken up from you into heaven shall so come in like manner as ye have seen Him go into heaven"**
> **(Acts 1:10-11)**

BOOK SUMMARY

The invitation to Christ's Salvation should not be complicated. It should be simple but not simplistic. Just what does it mean to be saved? Or to be born again? This book answers just that - not once, not twice but in virtually every chapter. There are, in my estimation, five categories of people in Church today, but just one category of people are saved.

1. The people who have no clue what the new birth (salvation) is, though they might have repeated the sinner's prayer at an altar call.

2. The people who have heard the message of Salvation but refused to decide to accept because they do not want to commit to anything that will make them accountable.

3. The people who heard and invited Jesus into their hearts, who thought the experience was too easy and too simple to be called Salvation. They go about with skepticism.

4. The people who do not understand the message of the cross because they have been presented with a complicated message of Salvation.

5. The people that are truly saved and are living the Christian life. This book will be of help to all readers- an eye-opener and a kind of prompter to lead the unregenerate (unsaved) to Christ and a useful tool and resource for personal evangelism to the one who is born again. The good savior and our Lord Jesus through the Holy Spirit have confirmed my one and consistent prayer about this book with a prophecy by a woman of God who did not at that time know that I was writing a book: that I would write a book on salvation, and no one who reads it will ever remain unsaved.

ABOUT THE AUTHOR

DR. OLUSOLA ISRAEL FADARE fondly called Olu Fadare is the founder and General Overseer of Living God Miracle Ministry, A.K.A THE LIVING GOD MINISTRIES in Queens New York, Tampa Florida (USA), Nigeria and Kenya, both in Africa. He is a versatile writer and graduate of English and creative writing, a product of four American Universities and colleges, he also holds a Doctoral Degree in Theology after he was called into ministry.

As he is fondly called, Olu is married to Mercy, co-founder of Living God Miracle Ministry. The couple had been residing in New York for over 30 years before recently moving to Tampa Florida, the new Headquarters of the ministry. They are blessed with four grown up children.

www.ingramcontent.com/pod-product-compliance
Lightning Source LLC
LaVergne TN
LVHW010555070526
838199LV00063BA/4975